TAYLOR

ERA BY ERA

TAYLOR

ERA BY ERA

THE UNAUTHORIZED BIOGRAPHY

CAROLINE SULLIVAN

Andrews McMeel
PUBLISHING®

Andrews McMeel Publishing
a division of Andrews McMeel Universal
1130 Walnut Street, Kansas City, Missouri 64106

www.andrewsmcmeel.com

First published in Great Britain in 2024 by
Michael O'Mara Books Limited

24 25 26 27 28 LAK 10 9 8 7 6 5 4 3 2 1

ISBN: 978-1-5248-9634-8

Library of Congress Control Number: 2024940698

ATTENTION: SCHOOLS AND BUSINESSES
Andrews McMeel books are available at quantity discounts with bulk purchase for educational, business, or sales promotional use. For information, please email the Andrews McMeel Publishing Special Sales Department: sales@amuniversal.com.

Contents

Introduction

Twenty years into Taylor Swift's career, it's hard to describe her success without reaching for superlatives. Performing for 70,000 people at a time and reaching No. 1 on charts around the world every time she releases an album are all in a day's work for her; she's won the Grammy Award for Album of the Year an unprecedented four times—and her influence extends well outside her own domain. How many other musicians have prompted a US Senate investigation into the concert-ticketing industry? Who else could impel film studios to change the release dates of upcoming movies to avoid clashing with hers? Who was the first musician ever chosen in her own right as *Time* magazine's Person of the Year?

In 2021, *Elle* labeled Swift "a pop megastar at celestial echelons," which comes as close as anything to capturing her status. In less galactic terms, as far as this pop megastar is concerned, records exist to be broken, targets to be surpassed—and she's still in her early thirties.

But even Swift herself must have been impressed by what she pulled off in a single two-week period in October 2023. Three major milestones were reached, and what the *Guardian* called "the shock of her vast stardom" became that much more vast. It feels right to begin this book by mentioning them, because Taylor Swift isn't just the twenty-first century's biggest artist; now she's also known for some of the smartest business decisions ever made by someone whose trade, technically, is writing and singing songs. This isn't *Taylor: The Business Manual* (though, don't bet against that book being written someday), but her acumen is a major part of who she is. It will influence the generations that follow as much as her music will.

The first milestone was reached on October 12, when the concert film *Taylor Swift: The Eras Tour*, composed of footage from three stadium shows in California two months earlier, was released. On presales alone, it was the highest grossing concert film ever made and looks set to become one of the most successful films of any genre. (Note: the opening date was changed from October 13 at the last minute by Swift herself, releasing a day early, and with a number of additional showtimes, to try to cope with the unprecedented demand for tickets.)

On October 26, Bloomberg reported that she had become a billionaire. Its "conservative" estimate was that she was, at that point, worth $1.1 billion, a good portion of it amassed from the ongoing Eras Tour, which began in March 2023 and concludes in December 2024.

Finally, on October 27, the *Taylor's Version* re-record of her 2014 album *1989* was released—the fourth in her highly successful series of re-recorded albums. Her self-proclaimed "favorite re-record," it sold 1.6 million copies in the US in less than a week—enough to make it the biggest album of the year there by some way. Accompanying the LP was a handwritten note released the same day on her social media channels: "I was born in 1989, reinvented for the first time in 2014, and a part of me was reclaimed in 2023 with the re-release of this album I love so dearly."

The business world has already noted her skill at running her career; sites like Forbes and Bloomberg watch her because she's a source of stories relevant to their readers. For instance, she illustrated good employer–worker relations by handing out bonuses totaling $55 million to the entire touring party on the Eras Tour (the truck drivers alone reportedly received $100,000 each), while the tour itself provides a lesson in supply and demand. On the first US leg (March–August 2023), there were plenty of enterprising touts charging up to $1,500 for a $50 ticket, but fan-to-fan resale sites also sprang up, matching those wanting tickets with ticket holders willing to sell their spares at face value.

On the basis of the summer 2023 gigs alone, Eras was the second highest grossing tour of all time, at $780 million. At that point, only Elton John's farewell jaunt was ahead—and by early 2024, Eras had surpassed it with its 151 shows grossing $1.03 billion. The icing on the tour cake is that the US dates are thought to have contributed $4.6 billion to the US economy thanks to, for example, soaring hotel room occupancy rates in each city she played.

Then there's her instinct for picking the right projects—an intuition that has been so unerring it should be known as

Taylor Swift Capitalism, suggested Sky Society, a media company aimed at women in marketing. Eras is an example. It's her first post-lockdown tour, which makes it the first chance for fans to hear the three albums (*Folklore, Evermore,* and *Midnights*) she recorded during the COVID-19 pandemic. Thus, desire to see her already existed and she cannily amplified it by announcing that Eras would be the first tour in which she played songs from all of her eras, or albums. (For reasons unexplained, her debut album isn't part of the show, though several songs, including "Tim McGraw" and "Our Song," have popped up in the nightly "surprise" slot.)

Taylor Swift Capitalism also saw the *Taylor's Version* re-records of her albums released to even greater acclaim (and often sales) than the original versions. She started the project in order to regain control of her master recordings after she left her former label Big Machine Records (more on this in Chapter 9). Her primary motive is demonstrably personal—she's reclaiming her artistic property—rather than mercenary. Yet she might just have had an idea that fans—the unswervingly loyal Swifties—would stand with her and buy the re-recordings. She was right. The Swifties have piled in, sending each of the first four *Taylor's Version* albums to No. 1 in the US and UK, Australia, Canada, Ireland, and New Zealand. "At its core this is a morally upstanding business exercise if ever there was one," Rachel Aroesti wrote in the *Guardian.* And if Swift gave herself a pat on the back when the *1989* re-record achieved the highest one-week US sales of any album since Adele's *25* in 2015, who could blame her?

The Haas School of Business at the University of California, Berkeley, went a step further in acknowledging her business sense. In autumn 2023, it announced a thirteen-week course for the spring 2024 semester entitled Artistry and Entrepreneurship: Taylor's Version. The inspiration behind the course was her ability to connect with fans; the Swiftie/Swift bond has made the artistry and entrepreneurship possible because of the fans' consistent encouragement. The syllabus describes the class as an exploration of "how art and authenticity create enduring value and a viable enterprise." Economics, business, sociology, and literature, as pertaining to Swift, will be studied, and students get two credits for participating. She joins Madonna, who was once the subject of an academic strand known as Madonna Studies, as one of the few musicians to warrant a structured college course.

The Haas announcement followed a similar one from Queen Mary University of London. A course called Taylor Swift and Literature will be taught at Queen Mary Summer School beginning July 2024. Though not business-focused, it offers an opportunity to reflect on how Swift became a cultural touchstone. The course takes the view that Swift's work is indeed literature and should be read as such. It's pitched as a study of "formal elements such as rhyme and word choice" and analysis of her songs "with the help of key texts in critical theory [to discuss] the political, national, and historical contexts of her work."

Confirmation, then—if it were needed—that Swift is more than a pop star, or even a mega pop star.

Together, the October milestones made Swift a subject of international conversation. Her current (as of this writing) partner, Travis Kelce of the Kansas City Chiefs football team, says he's "never dated anyone with that kind of aura about them." Coming from a star player who's no stranger himself to performing in stadiums in front of 70,000 fans, that's saying something.

But then, his fame and hers are on different levels. His agility on the field, which includes breaking an NFL receiving-yards record in November 2023, has won him scores of accolades, and three Super Bowl rings. Swift, on the other hand, inspired reams of media coverage just for liking a congratulatory post on the Chiefs' Instagram account: "[Kelce is the] fastest tight end to 11k receiving yards AND the only player in franchise history to do it."

This is a girl who grew up on a Christmas tree farm in Pennsylvania, whose goals were small and personal even after she became famous. Take, say, the moment in 2010 when she decided she must be doing pretty well because her *Speak Now* album was on sale at her favorite coffee place, Starbucks. "You go to Starbucks and there's only, like, two CDs for sale. I felt like that would be a really big deal if they wanted to sell one of *my* CDs," she told the *New Yorker*. This was after *Speak Now* had already sold 1 million copies and topped the American chart. That was fine in itself, but as far as she was concerned, getting into Starbucks was proof that she was really getting somewhere.

If only she'd known then that further Starbucks joy was in her future. In the run-up to Christmas 2021, the chain would commemorate the release of *Red (Taylor's Version)* throughout the month of December by renaming her go-to drink, the grande caramel nonfat latte, Taylor's Version. Could there have been a more Swiftian way of being crowned Queen of Pop? And this queen has never forgotten where she came from.

Kindness, generosity, and relatability have been key to Swift's rise—traits that are still central to who she is.

Era by era, from her eponymous 2006 album onward, Swift has become increasingly significant and has reached the point where the word "icon" is not an exaggeration. This is her story.

CHAPTER I

In the Beginning

Taylor Alison Swift, as she was born, calls herself a girl's girl. Despite being named after a man—singer-songwriter James Taylor—that's exactly what she is: she's tirelessly supportive of her female friends, and especially of female musicians. She inspires young girls to write their own songs. Even her mother's choice of a man's surname for her daughter had a pro-female origin: Andrea Swift liked his music and thought a gender-neutral name would be helpful if her daughter wanted to establish a business career. Swift didn't find out the source of her name until she happened to tell Andrea that the song she most enjoyed singing in school chorus class was "Fire and Rain" by "a guy named James Taylor." Her mother replied, "It's really funny that you say that, because you're kind of named after him." Swift said, "That was the first time I was ever told I'm actually named after James Taylor."

The other name her parents had considered was Shelby, "but then they realized my name would be She'll Be Swift, and that kids might make fun of me," she revealed in 2016 while visiting young patients at the Memorial Sloan Kettering Cancer Center in New York. And it could have been worse: while pregnant, Andrea Swift regularly listened to a certain British rock band and might have decided that her firstborn would thrive as Def Leppard Swift.

She revealed the origin of "Taylor" at a 2011 headlining show at New York's Madison Square Garden, the city's largest indoor venue. The best thing about playing there, she said, was that "magical, magical" things might happen—such as James Taylor himself walking onstage. And just like that, a dapper, suited J. Taylor joined her, guitar in hand, and the two sang "Fire and Rain," which had established him as one of the giants of the early '70s singer-songwriter boom. When they finished, she sat back, open-mouthed with joy, and applauded him as the audience roared.

"They really like you, I think," she said. "I'm so glad you called," he replied. Coincidentally, while "Fire and Rain" was his first hit, only one of his singles reached No. 1 on the *Billboard* Hot 100—"You've Got a Friend," his 1971 cover of a song written by a woman, Carole King.

It's unsurprising that Swift's strongest bond, certainly as a performer, is with women. Her songwriting chimes with female experience, discussing the fluctuations of relationships and pinpointing moments of euphoria and shoulder-shrugging indifference in a way few other contemporary songwriters manage. She's always filled notebooks with observations, and the diaristic detail of her lyrics hits home. Actual handwritten diary entries, some dating back to when she was fourteen and practicing her autograph in case anyone ever asked for it, were included with the deluxe edition of the 2019 album *Lover.* Her friendships with women are warm, and she's loyal. It's inconceivable, for instance, that she would abandon a friend in a nightclub because some guy gave her the eye.

She's spoken many times of her gratitude for her circle of girlfriends, some of whom have been in her life since her school days. "What does seem possible and easy and comfortable is having this entire league of incredible girlfriends that I have," she told *Esquire* in 2014, a week before the release of the original *1989* album. "And I can trust them, and the reason I know I can trust them is because nothing true about me is being written in the press right now." (In other words, none of her close friends had divulged personal information about her.)

When she spoke to *Esquire*, she had no idea how *1989* would escalate her celebrity status, transforming her from highly successful country-pop singer to blockbusting pop star. She might have had an inkling that the album would sweep her to the next level, but she couldn't have foreseen, for example, alt-country star Ryan Adams making a full-length cover version of the entire album, or having to trademark a certain three-word phrase from lead single "Shake It Off" to stop it from being monetized by T-shirt sellers and the like. Country stardom, even the very top tier, just doesn't have the reach of top-flight pop fame.

At that point, in October 2014, she'd had plenty of experience of being written about, but after *1989* it became constant. Most of the coverage was—and remains to this day— about who she was dating, and it had already become so galling that she "just stopped dating people [for a while], because it meant a lot to me to set the record straight—that I do not need some guy around . . . in order to feel OK about myself. And I wanted to show my fans the same thing."

The operative phrase is "I wanted to show my fans," the girls and women who support her. It was young women, often still at school—as was Swift herself when she started out—whose devotion enabled her career to climb, rung by rung. By the time the Eras Tour began its victory lap around the world, some Swifties had kept faith with her for nearly twenty years. They'd stayed with her because she was relatable—they'd grown up with her and been through every era alongside her.

To put it another way, Swift is loved because she's human. Yes, she's gilded and beautiful, and suffused with the kind of glow only detectable in pop artists at the very peak of their powers—Beyoncé and Dua Lipa also radiate the same shimmer. Yet Swift is a fallible, real person, and her realness is never far from the surface. Imagine Beyoncé interrupting a show, as Swift once did, with the announcement: "I'm sorry, guys, but I just really have to blow my nose. I swear I'm gonna do this really fast, can you please scream to fill the awkward silence, please?" That's why she has a place in so many hearts.

The Swifties' support has never wavered, even during a 2016 blip when she seemed to be caught lying about approving a Kanye West song that mentioned her. Others did turn against her then, and the incident caused her to take time off from public appearances.

In brief, this is what happened: on the song "Famous"—lead single from his 2016 album *The Life of Pablo*—West said it was possible that he and Swift could have sex, then called her a "bitch" and claimed he was responsible for her fame. That was a reference to his interrupting her acceptance speech at the 2009 MTV Video Music Awards. Her song "You Belong With Me" had won Best Female Video, and West came onstage to tell an astounded Swift that Beyoncé's "Single Ladies (Put a Ring on It)," which was nominated in the same category, was "one of the best videos of all time." The ensuing media frenzy ensured that the moment has never been forgotten.

Swift had apparently known about the "sex" line in advance; the two had talked on the phone before he recorded "Famous" and he mentioned it. In a partial transcript of the phone call released by Kim Kardashian in June 2016, she said: "I mean, it's like a compliment, kind of." She felt it was "tongue-in-cheek." But that wasn't the contentious part of the song. The sticking point was the word "bitch." West—who claimed he'd intended it "affectionately"—said he and Swift had discussed it during the phone call, and that she had OK'd it. Swift confirmed that they *had* talked on the phone but denied approving "bitch."

In a 2020 tweet, her publicist, Tree Paine, said West's main reason for phoning Swift was to ask her to post a link to "Famous" to her millions of Twitter followers, which she declined to do. Seemingly, any discussion of the song's lyric was secondary to that. She was made to look dishonest when West's then wife, Kim Kardashian, appeared to verify her husband's version of events. Kardashian also seemed to believe that Swift was denying she ever spoke to West.

In March 2020, Swift was vindicated when the rest of the phone conversation was leaked, and it appeared that "bitch" had not been discussed. Going by the leaked call, West did ask to use her name in the song, and she agreed; she also agreed to the having-sex line. But she didn't agree to "bitch." She couldn't have—it didn't come up in their discussion. Kardashian tweeted on March 24: "They clearly spoke [on the phone] . . . Nobody ever denied the word 'bitch' was used without her permission."

The convoluted wrangle brought out the worst in many media sites, with some pouncing on the opportunity to lay into the previously "perfect" Swift. (She was popularly perceived as so flawless that *Rolling Stone* titled a 2009 interview, possibly sardonically, "The Very Pink, Very Perfect Life of Taylor Swift.") There were corrosive headlines: "When Did You First Realize Taylor Swift Was Lying to You?" and the meta-question, "When Did the Media Turn Against Taylor Swift?"

Ramping up the anti-Swift sentiment, even a long-ended relationship with Harry Styles in 2012–13 was being criticized as having been a publicity gambit—though if that were true, why hadn't there been hundreds of paparazzi shots of the couple's quiet moments together, as usually crop up when romances are really showmances? Where were the shots of Styles taking her for lunch at the Fortune City Chinese restaurant in his hometown, Holmes Chapel, Cheshire? No photos of that day exist beyond one taken by the owner and another posted on Twitter by a customer.

It hardly needs saying that the Kanye and Kim controversy, and revenge—in the form of even greater success and acclaim—must have been sweet. Looking back at that time in her life several years later, Swift was surprisingly benign, telling *Rolling Stone*: "You can't keep winning and have people like it."

And, all along, the Swifties had her back. If Swift was going through a hard time, the Swifties were there with her, empathizing. A review in *Rolling Stone* of a May 2023 show at MetLife Stadium in New Jersey described a woman who fell to her knees and cried throughout a ten-minute version of "All Too Well," a luminous post-breakup "memory" song lyrically steeped in autumn leaves, crisp air, and plaid shirts. The reviewer, Rob Sheffield, was sitting in the next row; moved by her tears, he called the woman "my goddamn hero."

That's not to say that her music only chimes with women. On the contrary: in his review of the trio of Eras shows at MetLife, committed Swiftie Sheffield proved that women don't have a monopoly on Swift fanship. He vividly described his emotional response to the concerts—crying, singing along— and said he was still wearing a friendship bracelet given to him before one of the shows by another fan, a stranger.

The Swiftie passion for friendship bracelets—not to be confused with the Bejeweled bracelet, a gold-link and gemstone piece that was briefly available from her online store—took off when she mentioned them in a track on the 2022 album *Midnights*, "You're On Your Own, Kid." A tradition quickly grew around them, with fans exchanging them in parking lots before concerts. Often, as noted by Sheffield, exchangers had never met before, so the gesture had special, heartfelt significance. His feature-length review called the three-hour-plus set not just a "catharsis" for Swift herself but "an emotional, epic Tay-pocalypse" for the fans.

Swift is aware of the particular impact of "All Too Well"— since its parent album, *Red*, came out in 2012, she's had more requests for it at gigs than any other track. When she put out *Red (Taylor's Version)* in 2021, Swifties helped propel the track to No. 1 in the *Billboard* Hot 100. In effect, the fans have taken ownership of the song—something she acknowledges. It was never intended to be a single or a video, she said in a 2021 interview put out by her record company, UMG. "But what was so crazy is that when it went out into the world, the fans just among themselves decided it was their favorite. They just sort of . . . claimed it as the most important song from *Red* . . . This song has turned into a story of what the fans did for [it]."

It was girls—specifically teenage girls—who gave her a career in the first place. When she began shopping for a record deal, aged thirteen, she encountered skepticism everywhere. She'd written songs since she was ten, and her family had moved from Pennsylvania to Nashville with the express intention of helping her start a career in country music. But positioning herself as a country singer in America's country music capital raised eyebrows and hackles. She might have been precociously talented and fiercely intelligent, and she might have had a genuine passion for the music, but in Nashville that made no difference. She was told by labels that a kid who wrote her own songs about tumultuous high school romances wouldn't sell to country music's core demographic—mid-thirties women who, in any case, preferred male singers.

If she wrote a few songs directed at that older female audience, the labels said they'd think about signing her. Or if she were willing to let more experienced songwriters do the writing, leaving her simply to sing the songs, they would consider that, too. What the labels hadn't anticipated was that there might be a much younger female audience who loved country music—as Swift herself did—and would relate to a singer-songwriter their own age who created deeply emotional songs about her own experiences.

It's not that the country industry had intentionally snubbed young women; rather, country artists had always written and sung for the over-thirties crowd because they assumed that adults were the only ones listening. Scott Borchetta, founder of Big Machine Records, which signed her in 2005, later told *Inc.*, "[Country wasn't] a teen format. At that time, it was a 25–54 demographic [and] younger females had struggled mightily. There really weren't any at that time." Even the handful of very young artists who reached the top tier, such as Tanya Tucker and LeAnn Rimes, were developed with adult listeners in mind—both were thirteen when their first hits landed, and the maturity of their voices and material was geared to speak to adults. Tucker's first hit, in fact, came with a song that could hardly have been less teen-friendly: it was "Delta Dawn," an eerie, stately ballad about a forty-one-year-old woman who never got over being abandoned by a man who'd promised to marry her.

And then there was Swift.

The high school boyfriend who left her behind to go to college ("Tim McGraw"), the enviably gorgeous classmate who's secretly bulimic ("Tied Together with a Smile")—the characters in Swift's songs were the kind every teenage girl recognized. There was the "redneck" she dated in freshman year but eventually dropped because of his arrogance—that, and because he refused to let her drive his pickup truck ("Picture to

Burn"). Every young woman has been there, and Swift's gift was being able to turn her situations into songs.

Thanks to that ability, when she realized that she and the guy she wrote about in "Tim McGraw"—his name was Drew—didn't have an "our song," she was able to write one. Note: She had never before had a boyfriend to write about. Drew was her first. Swifties have speculated that "A Perfectly Good Heart" and "Fifteen" are also about him. In fact, the latter is about her best friend, Abigail Anderson, but it also contains ambiguous lines about a boy the song narrator wanted to marry someday, so it's possible that Drew was on her mind.

Aptly, she titled her new song "Our Song" and sang it at her ninth-grade talent show. Understandable: Why keep it for just the two of them? She knew it was special, she said during an AOL interview, when kids from school approached her months after the talent show to say they loved the song she'd played all those months before. "And then they'd start singing lines of it back to me. They'd only heard it once, so I thought, 'There must be something here.'"

When "Our Song" was released as a single, in September 2007, it spent six weeks atop the Hot Country Songs airplay chart, propelled by recognition she had won for her two previous singles, "Tim McGraw" and "Teardrops on My Guitar." It was the song that paved her way to country stardom.

Why that particular one? Because the words are potently descriptive: she was "riding shotgun" in her boyfriend's car, her hair flowing loosely over her shoulders, the boyfriend steering with one hand and holding her heart with the other . . . She had an eye for tiny details, and knowing she was fifteen when she wrote it makes it all the more remarkable. Secondly, it's a song *about* a song—she confesses in the first verse that the two of them don't have a tune they think of as theirs. Then, the best bit: the chorus. In it, the boy says they do have a song. It's made up of the sounds he associates with their relationship—her voice on the phone, the screen door clicking shut, the rap of his knuckles on her window so her parents don't hear. Together, they compose "their song." It's poetic and imaginative, and she wrote it, she said later, in twenty minutes.

Third: the melody and arrangement, richly infused with fiddle and banjo, bounces along, complementing the southern inflections in her voice. For a girl from Pennsylvania, she had learned to sing like a Tennessean, and the joy in her twang was infectious. Lastly, the color-saturated video, directed by veteran country director Trey Fanjoy, vibrantly mixes scenes of Taylor lying in a field of flowers and her getting ready for a date—chatting on a peach-colored landline, admiring her newly polished nails—in a prom dress on a front porch, screen door visible behind her. That switches to a contrastingly monochromatic scene of her on a soundstage, wearing a black dress and playing a big silver guitar as her backing band, who look more like an '80s new-wave outfit in their black-and-white suits, add upbeat flourishes. The video deservedly won the Video of the Year and Female Video of the Year trophies at the 2008 CMT (Country Music Television) Music Awards.

"Our Song" was also helped along by Swift having endeared herself to thousands of George Strait and Brad Paisley fans by touring as the country superstars' opening act in 2007. Both Strait and Paisley played coliseums and arenas, and Swift was facing up to 20,000 people every night. How did she do? A review of Paisley's show in the *Calgary Herald* summed her up in one highly positive sentence: "Warming up for Paisley was cute and charismatic Taylor Swift, seventeen, whose charming set really won the house," while the *Times Herald-Record* was even more taken with her at the Bethel Woods Center for the Arts: "A spitfire named Taylor Swift took the stage . . . For a young performer, Swift had an awesome stage presence and showed what an amazing future she has in store." *C-ville Weekly*, reviewing one of her George Strait openers, compared her to Dolly Parton—or Parton's hair, anyway, noting Swift's "bouncing blonde curls," which comprised "roughly half her body mass."

By the time those reviews appeared, her first album era was well underway. Her debut, *Taylor Swift*, had come out on October 24, 2006. The standard edition was composed of "Our Song," "Tim McGraw," "Teardrops on My Guitar," and eight other songs, all of them written in her bedroom or during school. She wouldn't turn seventeen for another seven weeks. She didn't expect much of the record at first, telling *American Songwriter*, "After the first week, I thought to myself, 'I would be incredibly lucky to see this album certified gold. Or certified anything.'" She was speaking to the magazine in 2011, at which point the album had been certified five times platinum. By 2017, it was seven times platinum—7 million copies sold.

Contrary to her expectations, it actually took off very quickly. In January 2007, three months after release, it was already gold, and its first single, "Tim McGraw," was in the Top 10. Naming the song after one of the superstars of country music ensured it got attention, but its success was due entirely to her own efforts. This is where her age was pivotal. She might have been too young to write meaningful songs for thirty-five-year-olds, but she was exactly the right age to know her way around the social media channels that were beginning to become popular. That was another blessing for her and her label, Big Machine. Country labels weren't getting much traction in the digital world because older country fans didn't buy downloads. But teenagers did. So, in a promotional sense, she had all bases covered: she spent most of 2007 on concert stages, charming Paisley's and Strait's older crowds, while engaging online with people her own age and being rewarded by strong download sales.

She was already known in Nashville, where her high school friends were spreading the word—apart from a jealous clique, who ostracized her—but there was a far bigger potential audience out there and she knew how to contact it. Her parents had been savvy enough to register the domain taylorswift.com in 2002, but within a few years, the best way to reach people was via social networks. She was active on MySpace, which she joined on August 31, 2005. It was then the highest profile social site and was the launchpad for a number of superstars-to-be, including Adele, Arctic Monkeys, and Calvin Harris. She instantly saw its possibilities—more than that, she was the first country artist to fully engage with it. "Online is cool," she said in 2006. "It really brings people together. It gives people an outlet to communicate."

She would have done the same with Facebook, but until it opened to anyone over the age of thirteen in September 2006, it was restricted to college students only, and she couldn't get an account. Undaunted, her manager, Rick Barker, turned to the only recent student in Taylor's band, fiddle player Emily Poe, who'd attended Belmont University in Nashville. Poe was on Facebook and let Barker communicate with fans until Swift was eligible to join in her own right.

Sociable by nature, Swift used MySpace to connect with fans—posting songs, responding to questions, keeping them updated. The main pillar of her approach was treating her fans as friends. Her MySpace biography, clearly self-written, showed her to be funny and personable: "I love people who are nice to me. My middle name is Alison. I'm extremely tall [5 foot 11 inches]. Like, I'm that really tall person that is blocking your view at a concert." There was a lengthy list of the other things that made her tick—"in my spare time I like to conduct random baking experiments in my kitchen and write letters to people"—and all anyone had to do to be her friend, Swift said, was like her. That was easily done. She was so genuinely likeable, who wouldn't want to be friends? She was the girl next door, if the girl next door had a record deal and a gift for writing songs that were fragile and personal but also universal. By 2007, she had 350,000 MySpace friends; by 2009, it was over 1 million.

Ask any major pop singer-songwriter—Adele, Lewis Capaldi, or her close friend Ed Sheeran—how they clicked with the public and the answer will be the same: their songs were relatable. Swift's writing was inspired by situations in her own life, and the way she wrote about them chimed with every teenage girl. Even a girl who knew nothing about country superstar Tim McGraw could feel that Swift was describing any girl's life, not just her own. (The song isn't about McGraw himself but is instead a bittersweet memory of listening to one of his tracks with her soon-to-be ex-boyfriend. Though it's not mentioned by name, the song they listened to in real life was "Can't Tell Me Nothin'," from McGraw's 2004 album *Live Like You Were Dying*.)

That was the start of the artist-fan relationship that's been so critical to her success. But first things first . . .

CHAPTER 2

First Things First

Though Swift had an interest in performing from a young age, it wasn't her first ambition. That was something else entirely: she wanted to be a stockbroker. Her father, Scott, worked as one at Merrill Lynch—and has three generations of bank presidents in his family tree—and Andrea Swift had been a "really big business executive [who] worked at an ad agency" before having children, as Taylor told TV channel Great American Country. "She had a complete career of her own and was supporting herself." Thus, where other third graders at Wyndcroft School in Pottstown, Pennsylvania, aspired to be astronauts and ballerinas, Swift had other ideas. "I'm going to be a financial advisor!" she informed her classmates, though at that stage she wasn't entirely sure what a financial advisor did. She was attracted to the idea, though, because her father "lives and breathes [his work]."

He certainly did. For Scott, financial management wasn't just a job; it was a vocation. (Taylor once revealed that he would end conversations not with "Bye-bye," but "Buy bonds.") He became a client of Merrill Lynch in 1966, aged fourteen, when he used the proceeds of his lawn-mowing business to buy one share of stock. After receiving a business degree from the University of Delaware, he joined Merrill Lynch Wealth Management. Later, he founded The Swift Group, a Merrill Lynch division based first in Philadelphia and New York and latterly in Nashville.

"My dad is so passionate about what he does, in the way that I'm passionate about music," Taylor told a YouTube Presents Q&A session in 2011. He'd given her a grounding in personal finance when she was very young, telling her to save her money "or invest in utilities," and his enthusiasm rubbed off on his daughter: "I saw how happy it made him and I just thought, 'I can broke stocks.'"

Would stockbroking have been a good fit for her abilities? She's erudite and quick-witted and, as pointed out in the Introduction, financially astute. Added to that, if she'd decided to go into the field, she would have had expert advice right there at home. Indeed, her dad does dispense financial wisdom to his daughter—he's involved with a number of businesses she owns, such as real estate and merchandising ventures, and provides investment direction and oversight. He offers the same service to the company Taylor formed when she bought a private jet and an aircraft hangar. Meanwhile, both parents help run her 13 Management company.

Scott and Andrea married in February 1988 and were materially secure enough to ensure a comfortable upbringing for Taylor and brother Austin, who was born in March 1992. So comfortable, in fact, that it has to be labeled "privileged," which has rankled some. In 2015, Salon.com published a piece titled "Taylor Swift is not an 'underdog': The real story about her 1 percent upbringing that the *New York Times* won't tell you." The article went on to say: "Swift is the privileged daughter of wealthy plutocrats. She can write a good pop song, but also had a huge leg up."

The article took issue with *The New York Times* calling her an "underdog" in a review of a show on the *1989* World Tour. In the *NYT* reviewer's opinion, Swift's celebrity was a disadvantage; she was so successful that she was uncool, and in music-scene terms uncoolness is a capital offense. The reasoning goes: if millions of people get excited about an artist who happens to sing pop songs, the artist must be inauthentic—appealing to more than a handful of people means that music snobs can't claim ownership of that artist.

So her "underdog" status in the *NYT* review was bestowed by the fact that she's enormously popular. In the world of "serious" music appreciation, her cultural "worth" had been decided by people whose own self-worth was wrapped up in the kind of music they allow themselves to listen to. Salon argued that genuine underdogs were musicians who came from impoverished backgrounds or those who, despite touring and releasing music regularly, couldn't make a living from it. But an artist doesn't have to be niche and living in hardship to count as an underdog. Arguably, even ABBA were underdogs for the first twenty years of their career, when they were selling millions of records but their music's artistic brilliance was dismissed by many as schlocky fluff. Happily, their pop genius is now widely acknowledged.

The *Times* quoted a line from the 2012 single "We Are Never Ever Getting Back Together," in which Swift accuses an ex-boyfriend of musical elitism. The lyrics say that the ex, whose identity she's never revealed (it was rumored to be Jake Gyllenhaal), would rather listen to some hipster indie album than one of his own girlfriend's records. His behavior would ring a bell with anyone who knows a dedicated fan of obscure bands—it's de rigueur for such types to sneer at pop, though they make occasional exceptions for a few critically approved acts. (An example of this is Girls Aloud, whose excellence even the most hardcore pop-avoiders didn't dispute.)

"It was a relationship where I felt very critiqued and subpar," Swift told the *Guardian*. "He'd listen to this music that nobody had heard of . . . but as soon as anyone else liked these bands, he'd drop them. I felt that was a strange way to be a music fan. And I couldn't understand why he would never say anything nice about the songs I wrote or the music I made." Her primary motive for writing "Never Ever" was to "absolutely drive him crazy" because he would hear it endlessly on the radio, and if that weren't bad enough, it would be the antithesis of "the kind of music that he was trying to make me feel inferior to," she told *USA Today*.

Revenge was hers. The song, written in twenty-five minutes by her and Swedish writer-producers Max Martin and Shellback, sold 6 million copies in the US, and was her first single to reach No. 1 on *Billboard*'s Hot 100 chart.

In the course of trying to put Swift in her place, the Salon article also noted that she "got a convertible Lexus" during her sophomore year in high school, apparently implying that it was a gift from her rich parents. It was an SC430, which cost $65,355 in 2006—a pricey status symbol, but it wasn't a gift. Swift bought it herself, with her earnings from music. The backstory is rather touching, highlighting her vulnerability. She was bullied at school by a group of girls who envied her growing success in music but simultaneously scorned it because it stemmed from country music, which was then about as uncool as it was possible to get. "A lot of girls thought I was weird," she told *Women's Health*. "Actually, the word they liked to use was 'annoying.' I'd sit down at their lunch table and they'd move to another one." They told her she had frizzy hair and laughed when she came to school with bandaged fingers incurred while practicing twelve-string guitar.

The girls were obsessed with *Mean Girls*, the 2004 film about high school social cliques; they particularly identified with the top clique, the shallow, bitchy Plastics. (Swift is also a huge fan of the movie, which came out when she was fourteen, and she can quote long sections of dialogue.) The queen of the Plastics, Regina George, owned an SC430, so Swift went for the same one, "as a kind of rebellion against that type of girl."

She got emotional as she spoke to the *Guardian* about that time in her life. The girls had never invited her to parties or shown any interest in getting to know her; she saw them as defined by materialism and gossip. "[They were] obsessed with that car and that girl and what the Plastics wear and how they talk . . . And instead of going to parties I've been writing songs and playing shows and getting these really small pay checks that have added up and now I get to buy a car—and guess which one I'm going to buy? The one that the girl you idolize has." They ostracized her, so she hit them where it hurt.

There was a postscript to all the drama: several years later, when she was playing a show, many of those same girls turned up in Swift T-shirts, wanting to catch up with their successful former classmate. Swift realized that they didn't remember bullying her and resolved to move on from any lingering bitterness she felt. Later, in a 2008 live chat, she was philosophical about her lack of popularity at school. "All the successful people I've met were not popular in high school. I've not met one successful person that was popular in high school. It's kind of like a badge of honor, when you graduate, to say that you weren't cool in high school."

Swift has been singing since the age of three, though genetic predisposition arguably played a part in her talent, too—her maternal grandmother, Marjorie Finlay, was an opera singer. She died in 2003, leaving Taylor regretting the opportunities she had missed to know her better. Taylor commemorated her on the 2020 album *Evermore*; the song "Marjorie," softly sung over a subdued electronic backing, movingly conveyed Swift's guilt and her feeling that her grandmother was in some sense still with her. A clip of her grandmother's coloratura soprano provided a haunting coda as the song played out. Marjorie got a credit on the album and the video: "Backing vocals: Marjorie Finlay."

Young Taylor also became an enthusiastic writer. An elementary school teacher once assigned the class a two-sentence essay; Taylor's filled two pages. Her teacher told her parents that she had never met a child like her.

Despite her stockbroking aspirations, it became clear that Swift was going to be a performer of some kind. Surprisingly, it was acting rather than music that first captivated her. She took acting lessons in New York and appeared in *Bye Bye Birdie, Annie, Grease,* and *The Sound of Music* at the Berks Youth Theater Academy.

By then, she was living in Wyomissing, a prosperous small town (or "borough," as it's designated) in southeastern Pennsylvania. The Swifts moved there in late 1997, shortly before Taylor's eighth birthday. Until then, the family lived on Pine Ridge Farm—an eleven-acre Christmas tree nursery in Cumru Township near the city of Reading. Her father had bought the place from a client before he met Andrea and ran the farm as a hobby, in addition to his Merrill Lynch day job. It was a serious hobby—he got up four hours before work so he could tend the fields on his tractor, and at Christmastime he sold the trees.

Taylor was born on December 13, 1989, in the nearby town of West Reading, and spent her early years on the farm. The countryside around it is outstandingly beautiful—it's horse country, and the Swifts had seven. Taylor rode competitively when she lived there, telling *Rolling Stone* in 2009: "I had the most magical childhood." From the age of five, she helped out during tree season. Each Swift had a job, and because she was too small to help hoist the Douglas firs onto car roofs, she was assigned the task of clearing praying mantis pods off the branches. Once she forgot, and the consequences were grisly: "They hatched all over these people's house. And there were hundreds of thousands of them," she told Jay Leno.

Her room was upstairs in a corner of the cozy farmhouse. Every bedtime—another pointer toward her future career—she insisted on being read three stories and singing five songs, typically from Disney movies. It sounds like an idyllic life, an impression supported by a picture she posted on Instagram in December 2019. There she was, perhaps a year old, with her parents at the farm. She was tucked between a smiling Andrea and Scott, next to a wooden Pine Ridge sign, and the three Swifts plus the family Doberman make a harmonious picture of family life.

She'd dug the photo out of the family album to promote a new song, "Christmas Tree Farm," which she wrote, recorded, and released in the first week of December. Its warm, nostalgic lyric paints a picture of festive ribbons and sleigh rides, holly and cider—the kind of Norman Rockwellesque family Christmas that Swift actually lived.

"Rockwellesque" also applied to the Swifts' summer home, a New England–style white house in Stone Harbor, New Jersey, which they owned from around 1992 until 2005. It was on the Jersey Shore, but many miles removed geographically and culturally from the *Jersey Shore* TV series. Behind the house was Sanctuary Bay; at the front, the Stone Harbor Bird Sanctuary, where Taylor watched feathery wildlife through binoculars. Otters slept on their dock at night, and a dolphin swam into the basin at the back; beyond the sanctuary was the Atlantic Ocean. The "little harbor town" at the far southern tip of New Jersey "was where most of my childhood memories were formed," she told *Vogue*. They were magical, those summers, and they exerted an effect on the dreamy, painterly songwriter she became. She spent some of the later summers playing little acoustic sets at the Coffee Talk café. An early unreleased song, "Smokey Black Nights," captured the feeling of those summers with its hazy verses about driftwood, tides, and constellations.

The move to Wyomissing, where the family bought a five-bed, three-and-a-half-bathroom, Colonial-style house built in 1929, meant swapping open countryside for town life. It wasn't too bad a trade—the house was a beautiful white clapboard with black shutters, brimming with period detail such as a butler's pantry and brick fireplaces. By then, Swift had found country music in the form of a LeAnn Rimes CD—a definitive moment that would set the course of her eventual life as a singer. Though only six when she discovered Rimes—who was just thirteen herself when the 1996 album *Blue* brought her nationwide fame—she instantly felt drawn to her storytelling. Rimes became a touchstone, spurring her to explore music.

More than that, Rimes was the direct inspiration for her decision to become a country artist. Swift can pinpoint the exact moment. When she was about seven, she went to see Rimes live in Atlantic City, New Jersey—it was her first concert, making it all the more memorable—and had an epiphany. "I was holding up this huge banner in the front row—'I love you LeAnn,' like a stalker," she said in a 2006 radio interview. Swift had written Rimes fan letters, and the night before the show she sent a package of drawings, along with a couple of photos of herself, to the singer's hotel.

"I had a huge blond 'fro so she recognized me in the audience," Swift remembered. Even better—miraculously—Rimes had taken the time to read her letters. She came to the edge of the stage to shake hands with fans, and when she reached Taylor, the seven-year-old asked if she'd received the letters. She said, "I sure did, Taylor"—a moment of kindness that changed Swift's life. In that moment "it all just clicked for me. If

I could ever make one little kid feel the way she made me feel, then it would all be worth it."

Years later, Rimes still remembered her seven-year-old fan. "She used to come and hold up signs, like 'I love you, LeAnn.' Crazy to see [how well] she's done. It's amazing," she told Virgin Radio in 2023. She hasn't worked with Swift but would love to: "I'm sure we could make that happen."

From that point, the only music that interested Taylor was country—specifically, female-led country. She was in luck, because the '90s were a fertile time for country crossover hits: in short order, she discovered Faith Hill's "This Kiss," Shania Twain's "That Don't Impress Me Much," "You Were Mine" by the Dixie Chicks (now known as The Chicks), and Martina McBride's "Wrong Again." Swift was attracted to both the stories in the songs and the singers' individual strength and self-determination.

(McBride returned the compliment in 2013, when she played a show at Nashville's Bluebird Café with the Warren Brothers. During the set they covered Tim McGraw's No. 1 single "Highway Don't Care," which featured Taylor on backing vocals. Andrea Swift was in the Bluebird audience that night, joyously swaying to the song, and she rose from her seat to sing the chorus. Afterward, McBride posted a video clip on Facebook: "Hey, Taylor Swift! You have the coolest mom! Check her out singing with me and The Warren Brothers!")

Compared with her love of country music, acting in Berks Youth Academy musicals didn't provide the same satisfaction. She was still taking acting lessons in New York—a 130-mile drive from Wyomissing—and had begun to audition, unsuccessfully, for Broadway shows. The idea of pursuing an acting career was starting to pall, especially as she was coming to realize that her favorite thing about working with the Youth Academy wasn't being onstage but going to the cast parties afterward. There was a karaoke machine, and once she discovered the delights of singing to music, her mindset underwent a definitive shift.

Years later, she said that when she was a kid, singing country karaoke gave her more joy than anything she had previously known. It was then, also, that people began to detect a country twang in her voice. Presumably, it had come directly from listening to the likes of Faith Hill and the Dixie Chicks. Pennsylvania didn't have much of a country scene; moreover, the largest city in the southeastern region where Taylor grew up was Philadelphia—famous for soul, rap, and rock, but absolutely not country. So while she spoke with a generic Pennsylvania accent, she sang with a twang. "It just came out sounding country, [because] it was all I had listened to," she told Great American Country.

A couple of years later, aged eleven, she was honing her karaoke style every Friday night at the Pat Garrett Roadhouse, a bar twenty miles north of Wyomissing. Garrett ran a weekly competition, the prize being the chance to play a gig with his own band. Doggedly signing up to sing at the Roadhouse week after week, Swift finally won the contest. Garrett, a sheep rancher and country singer in his own right, let her sing two songs with his group at the Bloomsburg Fair, a long-established agricultural event in Bloomsburg, Pennsylvania, in September 2001. "Ladies and gentlemen, we have a young lady who's going to be a big country star one of these days," he told the audience, more presciently than he knew. "Put your hands together for Taylor Swift!'

Still three months from her twelfth birthday, Taylor—long blonde hair, microphone in hand, absolutely fearless—sang LeAnn Rimes's 1999 hit "Big Deal," and "Timber, I'm Falling in Love" by Patty Loveless. She was so assured that it didn't much matter whether she'd "lived" their storylines. In everyday life she probably hadn't accused a love rival of "bragging" about stealing her boyfriend ("Big Deal"), nor fallen like a tree—"Timber!"— for a new love. Country music, as she already knew, was about storytelling, and it didn't matter whether a singer had lived the story in real life as long as they could persuasively tell the story. Even at eleven, she did that.

Years later, Garrett told a CBS News interviewer that while Swift "wasn't the best singer" he'd ever come across, she had a crucially important quality: drive. Scott Swift had once shown him a spiralbound notebook belonging to Taylor that contained nothing but her signature, page after page of it—she was practicing her autograph, confident that now she had a foot in the door thanks to the Bloomsburg Fair appearance, she was going places.

On the subject of Swift's voice: Garrett could have been referring to her relatively narrow range and lack of flashy technique. Swift herself has said that "being widely and publicly slammed for my singing voice" instilled doubts about her own ability; in a note accompanying the 2023 release of *Speak Now (Taylor's Version)*, she revealed that she'd worked intensively on her vocal skills before recording the original *Speak Now* in 2010.

She had been fed up with detractors criticizing her singing and questioning whether she wrote her own songs—because who ever heard of a young female artist coming up with her own material? Dolly Parton, Lady Gaga, and Adele, to name three of hundreds, could have put the doubters right—all wrote, or sometimes co-wrote, their own songs almost from the start, and Swift's catalogue is notable for the number of tracks on which she receives sole writing credit.

So, working on *Speak Now*, she had been determined to challenge herself and "build on [her] skills as a writer, an artist, and a performer." Which she did. The pertinent thing isn't whether she has a melismatic, powerhouse voice, but what she does with the vocal cords she was born with. She tells a believable story and does it with great sensitivity; she also composes righteous melodies. That's more than enough.

Back in the early 2000s, though, Scott knew his daughter had something special and asked Garrett for advice. Garrett was well-placed to give it. Having recorded in Nashville and landed several songs in the country chart (the Arctic Monkeys also covered one of his songs, "Bad Woman"), he knew what he was talking about when he suggested Taylor be allowed to try her luck in the country music capital. "Three months later, he comes in my store, the Sheepskin Shop, and says, 'Well, we're going to Nashville.' [I said], 'Oh, that's nice, how long you going for?' Figuring it was two weeks. He said, 'The rest of our lives.'"

Scott's conversation with Garrett took place in 2004, a few years after Taylor played with him at the Bloomsburg Fair. He and the Swifts had kept in touch, and Taylor never forgot his faith in her. When her debut album had sold its first million copies—eventually it went seven times platinum—her parents presented him with a platinum disc. Long before that, however, when Taylor recorded a two-song CD in 2003 to sell at karaoke shows and small gigs at fairs—an autographed copy went for $5—she made sure to give one to Garrett. She wrote on the booklet: "To my favorite people," and signed it with a swooping T and S—the autograph she'd been practicing.

The CD, produced by New York producer Steve "Mr. Mig" Migliore, had two tracks: "Lucky You" and "Smokey Black Nights." The former was the first song she wrote, aged twelve, on the same day that she learned G, D, E, and A—her first four guitar chords. A local computer technician, Ronnie Cremer, taught them to her—according to Cremer, who spoke to the *New York Daily News* in 2015.

There are two versions of her guitar-learning story: Swift's and Cremer's. He had a computer repair shop and played guitar, and Swift says there was "this magical twist of fate" when he came to the house to fix her desktop PC. She already owned an acoustic guitar, a gift from her parents when she was about nine, but for several years it was merely an ornament, propped against her bedroom wall, because her fingers were too small to play it. In the 2010 documentary *Taylor Swift: Journey to Fearless*, she remembered Cremer (pronounced "Cray-mer") arriving while she was doing her homework and asking whether she played that guitar in the corner. She told him she'd tried but hadn't gotten anywhere. "He said, 'Do you want me to teach you a few chords?' I said, '*Yes!*'" And from that moment, she was "relentless about wanting to play all the time. I was songwriting for all of my free time after that."

In a 2009 interview on the UK music series *The Hot Desk*, Swift gave a slightly different account of that impromptu lesson. She said Cremer brought a guitar along when he came to fix the computer, because he had just come from a show. He asked if she wanted to learn a few chords, and she said she would. He taught her several and left the guitar with her for a week so she could practice. She wrote her first song, "Lucky You," that first night. Swift laughed, "The computer was fixed and also I found what I wanted to do with the rest of my life." Cremer returned every week to show her new chords, and she progressed quickly.

Then there was Cremer's own recollection, as related in the mid-2010s. "I was the infamous, or famous, computer teacher that taught Taylor how to play guitar," was how he introduced himself in a video interview for the *New York Daily News*. He had a small recording studio within his computer shop in Leesport, eleven miles down Route 222 from Wyomissing, and one day circa 2001 his brother, Kirk—who was involved with the Berks County Youth Academy—came in with Taylor, Andrea, and Austin Swift. Taylor wanted to make a demo and asked if Cremer would help her record a couple of cover versions. "Once the demo went through and that seemed to work out pretty well and we got a bit of a comfort zone for each, they asked me to give her lessons." He was more into rock than country but was able to instruct in the technical side of playing—theory, song structure, and projection. The first song he taught her was Cheap Trick's "I Want You to Want Me," which she later played in her live shows. "When she started piecing songs together, that was when I started seeing somebody who really wanted to work."

Note: Kirk Cremer ran a *Saturday Night Live*–inspired group called Theater Kids Live! and, sensing potential, invited Taylor to join the group. He felt she had a natural affinity with comedy, but her presiding interest was music. She didn't join Theater Kids, but Kirk worked with her as a vocal coach, developing her clear but untutored voice. He carried out managerial-type duties, too, such as arranging for headshots to be taken for her portfolio and even going to a few Broadway auditions with her. Though the acting didn't bear fruit and music was now her priority, she remained interested in stage productions, commenting to *Inquirer Entertainment* that she'd "never lost my passion for theater." A what-if? game presents itself here: What if one of the auditions had resulted in a role and acting became her predominant focus? Would she have picked up that guitar a couple of years later?

Though Ronnie later did computer work for the Swifts, he maintained that his first visit was expressly arranged to teach Taylor to play guitar. She was then twelve, and he worked with her on Tuesdays and Thursdays from 5 to 8 p.m., earning $32 an hour. "In all honesty, I thought she was a pretty good student," he said. After a while, they incorporated the Ableton Live songwriting and recording computer program into the lessons. Cremer told her it was useful for structuring songs—the verse goes here, the chorus there—and she quickly picked it up. After *Taylor Swift* came out, Cremer said Scott Swift sent him a platinum disc, and the family also gave him a guitar worth $5,000.

In the meantime, though, there was that very first song, "Lucky You," written the same night Cremer taught her those first chords. It's hopeful and optimistic, and the lyric shows that, even at twelve, Swift was an observational writer. The subject of the song, a girl called Lucky, is different from others in her town and relishes it. She carries a rabbit's foot and dances with joy, considering herself lucky to be who she is. There's a lot of Swift in the Lucky character. Later, she was slightly apologetic about it being a "very twelve[-year-old's song]" and compared her voice to a chipmunk's, but she was still proud enough to call it "so sweet."

Swift describes many events in her life as "magical," and to her, Nashville is a magical place. Because two of her favorite singers, Faith Hill and Shania Twain, launched their careers there, she was desperate to visit. Visit? She actually wanted to move there, without ever having seen the place, and to her—if nobody else in her family—it was a foregone conclusion that it would happen. "I decided to move to Nashville when I was about ten years old," she told *Time*.

From babyhood, she'd been told by Andrea that she could achieve anything she wanted, as long as she put in the work. And that was precisely what she did once she decided that she had to live in Nashville. "I began absolutely nonstop tormenting my parents, begging them on a daily basis to move there," she told the *Daily Telegraph*. After a solid year of pleading, she half-got her wish. Even the resoundingly supportive Scott and Andrea weren't about to pack up their lives on a whim, but during spring break in 2001, Andrea Swift took Taylor, who was eleven, and her brother to Nashville for a look around. They arrived at the airport, rented a car, and headed straight for Music Row, where the country music industry conducts its business in atmospheric nineteenth-century warehouses and storefronts. Andrea waited in the car while Taylor darted in and out of publishing and label offices, handing receptionists copies of a demo CD of songs by Dolly Parton, LeAnn Rimes, and the Dixie Chicks that she had covered. She would introduce herself—"My name is Taylor and I'm eleven"—and explain that she was there to get a record deal. Each visit lasted four or five minutes, if that; after she announced her purpose, she confidently added, "Call me."

She had an idea that her gumption would be rewarded with a deal there and then. It didn't happen. "I think I had, like, one person call me back. And he was so sweet, just kind of telling me, 'You know, this is not how you do this,'" she told Great American Country. But the disappointment taught her a lesson: everyone in Nashville wanted a record deal, and submitting karaoke demos revealed her lack of readiness. To compete, she'd have to write her own songs and play guitar (hence the lessons from Cremer starting around that time). A few years later, talent shows like *American Idol* would upend the idea that aspiring stars needed original material—its first country-genre winner, Carrie Underwood, swept the 2005 series by singing cover versions week after week. But in 2001 Nashville, originality was as important as talent. Taylor had the talent. Now she set about learning to be a singer-songwriter.

She got the guitar lessons and practiced four hours a day; she mastered the twelve-string guitar, and she learned to write songs. Illustrating the strides she had made, two of her very earliest songs—"The Outside" and "Christmas Must Be Something More," both written when she was twelve—were good enough to be on her debut album and a Christmas EP, respectively. She began to play at coffee shops, learning how to perform in front of audiences.

During the next year or so, she returned to Nashville every two months, "trying to meet songwriters, trying to get my foot in the door," she told CMT News. Other things were happening, too. In the late summer of 2002, she beat dozens of other young singers at a US Open Casting Call—the prize was being the one to perform "America the Beautiful" for 24,000 tennis fans at Arthur Ashe Stadium in New York. In April 2002, she also sang the national anthem, "The Star-Spangled Banner," at a Philadelphia 76ers vs. Detroit Pistons basketball game at the First Union Center in Philadelphia. When she hit the song's crescendo—"O'er the land of the free and the home of the brave"—her voice was so strong that the spectators broke into applause. In a small, localized way, she was building a profile. And that day was memorable in another way: Jay-Z happened to be courtside, and when she finished, he high-fived her, giving her something to boast about for the next year.

An unintended consequence was that she became a singular figure at school, and as anyone who's ever been a kid knows, the worst thing to be is different from everyone else. "I got teased a lot and made fun of a lot, and went through periods of time when I didn't have friends," she remembered in *Taylor Swift: Journey to Fearless*. Andrea Swift's recollection of that time was equally bleak. While the other girls were having sleepovers, Taylor's ardent desire was to get up on a stage, and for that she was "shunned, ostracized." It didn't help that after she performed at the 76ers game, the local *Reading Eagle* wrote a piece about it, describing her "private dressing room" and the presents she received from the team, including a basketball and a jersey signed by some of the players. When she arrived at school the day after the story ran, the jealousy was almost physically palpable. "She would sit at a table with her lunch tray and everyone would move," Andrea said.

She continued the Nashville visits, which kept yielding the same frustrating results. When she occasionally made it past the front-desk receptionists and spoke to a label executive, she was rebuffed, over and over, for the same reason: kids didn't listen to country music. The only people who did were thirty-five-year-old women. There was no point signing her because she wouldn't get played on country radio. And on and on, always the same rejection—which Swift refused to accept. *She listened to country, didn't she?*

Finally, she met someone who thought the same way she did. On one of the trips—she was thirteen by then—she managed to arrange a meeting with A&R staff at RCA Records Nashville. She brought along her guitar and played, she later estimated, twenty songs. Then she played for RCA Nashville's chairman, Joe Galante, who was impressed enough to offer her a two-year development deal. It was September 2003. In *Journey to Fearless*, Swift defined a development deal: "Basically, it's 'We believe in you; we're going to watch you.' Not, like, 'You're making an album now.'"

It wasn't the deal she'd craved; in essence, RCA expected her to prove herself before she'd be allowed to record an album. But it was Nashville's first real show of interest in her—it was confirmation that this kid from Pennsylvania could be onto something.

CHAPTER 3

Fighting to Be Heard

Taylor kept writing songs, and she and Andrea took them to RCA as often as once a week, trying to show that she was ready to make an album. Each time, she was told she was becoming more skillful and the songs were approaching the standard the label expected. But there was no, "These songs are great! Let's make a record!"

When the first year was up, in September 2004, RCA wanted to take up the option for a second year. They would continue to watch her and pay for her to make demos, but there would be no promise of actually releasing a record. They also wanted the demos to be cover versions. There was an implication that the label wanted to wait at least a few more years before fully committing. As Taylor explained it to the *Telegraph*, "[They] announced they were going to shelve me, and 'monitor my progress' until I was eighteen." She was deeply disappointed, because not only had she written dozens of songs that proved her ability during the first year, she was also terrified that the sensitive storylines of songs she wrote as a young teen wouldn't keep. Their use-by date was there and then.

A month before the end of the first year, Swift made a perceptive observation to the *Press of Atlantic City*. "I don't want to be an adult country singer. I want to get out there as soon as possible. A young pop singer is fourteen years old. A young country singer is twenty-nine years old." Like every fourteen-year-old, she wanted to grab the moment, because if she didn't, the chance might never come around again. She genuinely felt she had no time to waste; if she didn't record these songs now, they would no longer reflect who she was, and she was staunchly opposed to faking emotions. She wasn't just opposed to it, she was constitutionally unable to do it.

"So I did something you don't usually do in Nashville when you have an in with a record label," Swift said in *Journey to Fearless*. "I walked away. Because I had a feeling I was not going to be able to record my own music." Her parents were aghast. Not only was she walking out on a major label and a deal that other young singers would have done anything to land, but Scott and Andrea had uprooted their lives for her.

The Swift family had moved to Nashville in April, five months before she left RCA. It was her parents' ultimate sign of commitment to their daughter's aspirations. Visiting the city every couple of months was burdensome, and once she was under contract to RCA, being based 780 miles from Nashville put her at a disadvantage when it came to being able to respond quickly when opportunities came up. Would Taylor have hurried down to serve as the "official entertainment" at the Nashville Rubber Duck Race if she'd had to travel for hours to get there?

The event was exactly as it sounded: thousands of numbered rubber ducks were launched into the Cumberland River and floated past as a fourteen-year-old Taylor performed on a pontoon moored to the riverbank at Riverfront Park. She landed the show thanks to a trade-off arranged by her father: Scott Swift was asked to "corral" 15,000 ducks—transport them in his boat to the race launch point—and he agreed on the condition that Taylor was allowed to perform. Scott was unable to watch her play, he said in an email to Taylor's manager, Dan Dymtrow; he was busy "picking up 15,000 ducks out of the river." At least he was able to say that his daughter had gotten "a very high-profile gig" out of it.

In 2022, chat-show host Graham Norton surprised her by showing a photo of the event, much to the audience's delight. Swift's own reaction was something less than unbridled joy. Looking at her teenage self gamely playing her acoustic guitar, backed by two other guitarists, a drummer, and a keyboardist, she said, "I think I've blocked a lot of this out." She wryly pointed out the "high concept" banner bearing her name—that was it, just a sign with her name across it, propped up in front of the pontoon.

RCA had told the Swifts to consider moving, and the advice was starting to make sense. The development deal proved that her parents' faith in her was justified—they were more than just "proud parents," as Andrea put it—and living in Nashville would give Taylor a chance to pursue music full time. That is, minus her school hours, because she was still a full-time student. The mildly tricky part was Scott's job—he commuted to Merrill Lynch's offices in Philadelphia and New York, and while the company (known just as Merrill from 2019) had a presence in Nashville, he didn't agree to the move until it was clear that he could successfully continue to run his Swift Group financial advisory service in Tennessee.

Scott and Andrea didn't want to move into Nashville itself, where Taylor's classmates would have been musicians' and label executives' kids. She was then in eighth grade, and because everything else in her life was changing so quickly, it was imperative that she had a sense of normalcy at school. They especially didn't want her to feel daunted by the wealth and connections of young Nashville royalty, while she was sitting in her bedroom after school every day writing songs that might or might not transform the development deal into a recording contract.

They moved to Hendersonville, eighteen miles northeast of Nashville—only half an hour from Music Row but far enough from the city to be a community in its own right. They bought a property on the shore of Old Hickory Lake—the same shore where Johnny Cash once lived, and not far from the house Roy Orbison built for his family in 1968. (His son, Roy Jr., said in a 2017 website post that he was saddened by Hendersonville's rapid expansion from a village of 700 people to "a giant suburb of apartment buildings.") The property had its own dock, which is what sold the place to Scott Swift. Before he and Andrea even looked at the house itself, they were down at the dock, so Scott could check the setup.

What he was hoping for was a place to berth his prized motorboats, and he got it. He'd owned a boat since the family began spending summers at Stone Harbor; in Hendersonville, there was room for two. They were a 420 Sundancer and a 220 Sundeck, both built by recreational-powerboat manufacturer Sea Ray. The forty-two-foot-long Sundancer can accommodate up to twelve passengers, while the relatively small Sundeck is twenty-two feet but can seat up to ten. The family made regular use of both; indeed, Scott persuaded Taylor to apply for a boating license when she was fifteen. "I have a license to drive a boat—I'm very proud of it," she told *People* in 2009. Maybe it was fitting that the first magazine cover of her career was a boating publication: *Sea Ray Living*, which featured the whole Swift family on the front of the spring 2006 edition.

"Meet Taylor Swift, sixteen-year-old daughter of Sea Ray owners Scott and Andrea Swift and a freshly signed country music artist," the text said. "We've grown up on Sea Rays. At the age of four, I lived in a life jacket," she told the magazine. Sea Ray boat owners saw themselves as a club, and the company built on that by publishing *Sea Ray Living* and hosting a unique music-and-boat festival called Aquapalooza. The clue is in the "Aqua"—the event, which is still held annually, got its name from the Lollapalooza music festival, but it couldn't be more different from that long-established Chicago gathering.

The slogan "Sea Ray's largest on-the-water boater celebration" sums it up: Aqua brings together thousands of boats and entertainers such as country singer-songwriter Alan Jackson, alternative rock band Everclear, and, several times, Swift; multiple Aquas are held each year at different locations—bays, beaches, marinas, or lakes—and some are simply waterborne get-togethers with no superstar entertainment. The larger ones are closer to the traditional idea of a music festival: the crowds—which can include intrepid pet dogs—eat, drink, and watch bands, and do so without having to buy a ticket, because the gatherings are free. When artists are playing on the floating stage, many fans swim closer to get a better view, and watch the sets standing waist-deep in the water, perched on plastic floats, or supported by rubber rings.

Hundreds of people did exactly that when Swift played in 2006 and 2007 (at, respectively, Fort Loudoun Lake in Knoxville, Tennessee, and Fairview Beach, Virginia), creating a sight she's not likely to witness at any other festival she plays. Arriving at the 2006 event, she filmed a brief clip for the organizers: "Hey, my name's Taylor Swift, we're in beautiful Knoxville, Tennessee, for Aquapalooza 2006. And I'm here because of [Knoxville country station] WIVK and Sea Ray—the best boat you will ever own. Be sure to watch the show." Then she climbed into a motorboat and was whisked to the floating stage. The date was July 22, a month after her debut single "Tim McGraw" had come out and three months before *Taylor Swift* would make its entrance. If she was there to plant a little seed of awareness in the minds of boaters—that this young woman is an up-and-coming star with a soon-to-be-available album—she also looked as if she were having fun doing it.

Swift's association with Hendersonville is now commemorated with a marker on East Main Street, part of a series called Tennessee Musical Pathways, which salutes the state's eminent artists. Though the marker has a photo of her holding three Grammy Awards at the 2016 ceremony (Album of the Year and Best Pop Vocal Album for *1989* and Best Music Video for "Bad

Blood"), her musical track record was only part of the reason she received the Pathways nod. The other was her generosity to both the local community and the state of Tennessee, in the form of large donations to projects ranging from the refurbishment of Hendersonville High School's auditorium, to repairing a playground damaged by a Cumberland River flood in 2010, to endowing an education center run by the Country Music Hall of Fame. A supporter of LGBTQ+ rights, she also contributed to the Tennessee Equality Project, a lobbying organization that advocates for LGBTQ+ people in the Tennessee General Assembly and local government throughout the state.

By the time the Swifts moved to Hendersonville, Taylor had a manager, Dan Dymtrow, who also worked with Britney Spears at that time. After Taylor sang at the US Open, the tournament's entertainment director, Kelly Foster, asked if she could send Dymtrow the twelve-year-old's demo CD. Dymtrow was impressed. He met Taylor and her parents, and after chatting to her and listening to her play, he was "completely blown away by her voice, intelligence, songwriting ability, and confidence," he told the *Reading Eagle*. "She was only thirteen years old in age but way beyond her years in talent and poise. She has the knowledge and intelligence of a thirty-year-old, and an extremely supportive family and group of friends." In January 2003, a month after Taylor's thirteenth birthday, he and the Swifts agreed that he would represent her.

She mentioned Dymtrow in the August 2004 issue of *Vanity Fair*, which gave her a full page in a Rising Stars feature sponsored by Abercrombie & Fitch. Photographed in A&F jeans and top, holding the neck of her guitar and dabbing at her eyes with a tissue—because writing love songs can be an emotional business—she said in the accompanying text: "After I sang the national anthem [note: it was actually a different song, "America the Beautiful"] at the US Open last year, a top music manager signed me as his client." She emphasized her love of country music, especially its baked-in tradition of telling relatable, human stories. "I sometimes write about teenage love but am presently a fourteen-year-old girl without a boyfriend," she said, with remarkable candor. She worried about it—was she wearing "some sort of guy repellent"? But at that stage of her life, having a boyfriend wasn't nearly as important as the music she was making—some of which was about, yes, boys—because she urgently wanted it to reach other people and move them.

The *Vanity Fair* story was a big deal; the nineteen-page A&F supplement featured Swift and twenty-seven other new faces deemed to have the making of future stars. Additionally, her photo was hung on Abercrombie shop walls. Not all of the twenty-eight have fulfilled expectations, but Olivia Wilde, Michelle Trachtenberg, and *Twilight*'s Nikki Reed have done pretty well for themselves. And Swift, of course, quickly became the biggest new star of the decade—though in August 2004, she was simply excited to be included.

Nine years later, however, she might have felt differently about Abercrombie, when the label put out a T-shirt poking fun at her love life. The shirt boasted that the wearer had had "#more boyfriends than t.s." While Swift didn't comment, some fans were irate at the implicit shaming and launched a Change.org petition, demanding that Abercrombie withdraw it. The petition, titled "Take away '#more boyfriends than t.s.' T-shirt," had a declarative section called "Why This Petition Matters," under which the organizer wrote: "Because it's hurtful to Taylor Swift and Swifties everywhere!"

Only 305 people supported it, but the Swifties' social power extends far beyond mere numbers. (Its only real fandom rivals are Army and Monbebe—the names adopted by followers of K-pop giants BTS and Monsta X. Some Monbebes have used the quote "We have limited capabilities but unlimited determination," from Chinese TV series *Meteor Garden*, to emphasize their fierce loyalty to the band.) The petition launched on June 18, 2013. Within days, calls to the company's PR department were answered thus: "If you are calling regarding the Taylor Swift T-shirt, please note that this is no longer available."

Swift had landed the A&F *Vanity Fair* spot when Dymtrow, hearing about the company's Rising Star campaign, sent over her press kit. He got a call back almost immediately. "I was just thinking, 'I'm not cool enough for this! I mean, it's Abercrombie & Fitch!'" Taylor told the *Nashville City Paper*. Indeed, Taylor didn't obviously fit the provocatively trendy image the label had fashioned for itself. It had started as a preppy outfitter but gradually won over the non-preppy dollar by opening shops in malls, using shirtless male hunks both in its advertising and on the actual shop floor and directing its marketing at high schoolers and college students, turning the brand into a status symbol. Its Abercrombie-logo sweatshirt was ubiquitous.

And, in something of a masterstroke, stores replicated a club atmosphere by dimming the lighting and playing loud music. The *Daily Mail* grumpily responded: "Why DO teen clothing chains insist we shop in the dark?" The answer was that Abercrombie (and its subsidiary, Hollister) wasn't insisting that "we," the newspaper's readers, shop in the dark; it was their trendy teenage children they were after. That's why country fan Taylor—not "trendy" in the slightest—thought she wasn't cool enough.

Clever Abercrombie: at one point, American teenagers voted it the sixth coolest brand. But it was also "exclusionary," said its then CEO Mike Jeffries, telling Salon in 2006 that the shops hired only attractive people because he wanted attractive customers. "We want to market to cool, good-looking people. We don't market to anyone other than that." He said that many people—the less cool and beautiful, presumably—"don't belong [in our clothes]. Are we exclusionary? Absolutely."

If Taylor was ever aware of his comments, she must have found them ironic. Two years earlier, she had appeared in the Rising Stars feature, this girl who had felt lonely and shunned at school and whose most pressing ambition was to touch people with her music. She'd thought she was too uncool to take part in the Abercrombie campaign, and here was Jeffries, in 2006, actually saying that the brand preferred "cool, good-looking people."

But by 2006, she was well on her way to achieving her goal. She has never mentioned Jeffries' "exclusionary" remark, but it was the kind of thing that was antithetical to what she believed in. In 2013, Jeffries issued a statement declaring Abercrombie's opposition to "derogatory characterizations . . . based on race, gender, body type, or other individual characteristics." He left the company in 2014.

Here it should be pointed out that Taylor was always attractive, even when she thought she wasn't; the fourteen-year-old in the Abercrombie story had a peachy, all-American appeal, even if she was then unable to see it herself. She was the archetypal wholesome, blue-eyed blonde, which didn't hurt at all while she was building her country career. To that end, in 2009 she even developed her own line of sundresses—the ultimate garment for country girls when they're kicking back in the summertime—which sold at Walmart for a highly wallet-friendly $14.

"These are my favorite things to wear," she told *Women's Wear Daily.* "When we were designing them, we had so many ideas to work from, and it came down to creating dresses that I would wear. If I couldn't see myself wearing them, I wasn't interested in making them." That was another big point in her favor: though her fans were mainly teenage girls, their mothers could also appreciate her. Not only was she exceptionally clean-cut—an important distinction at a time when some young female stars were rolling out sexualized new images—she had made it easy and affordable for fans to dress like her. In effect, she was every parent's dream pop star. In fact, they almost didn't make them like her any more. When she told *Unrated* magazine in 2007 that she had "never cheated on anybody or done drugs or gotten drunk," she sounded almost quaint, but it happened to be true.

One of her earliest songs was "The Outside," written when she was twelve and "a complete outcast at school. I was a lot different than the other kids and I never really knew why," she told *Entertainment Weekly.* There were two obvious reasons, which she herself mentioned at various times. One was that she was much taller than most of the girls, and even some of the boys, and kids can be intolerant of physical nonconformity. Never mind that she was also funny, a good person, and bright enough to be a member of the prestigious National Honor Society (former members: Michelle Obama, Meryl Streep), her height made her stand out. Secondly—yet again—she was a country fan. And not just a fan—she actually wrote country songs and wanted to be a country singer. In the eyes of her classmates, if she had sung opera like her grandmother Marjorie, she couldn't have been weirder.

And the problems encountered at Wyomissing Area Junior/ Senior High School followed her to Hendersonville High. By then the "country singer" issue was compounded by the fact that everyone else at school was listening to Alicia Keys, Usher (whose 8-million-selling *Confessions* was 2004's biggest-selling album), and The Killers' "Mr. Brightside" (which legendarily took on a life of its own, spending 382 nonconsecutive weeks in the UK singles chart as of October 2023). And while her classmates were plugged into their new fourth-generation iPods with their snazzy click wheels, Taylor was plugged into country music and "feeling" it far more than she did "younger" genres. That made her plain strange, as far as Hendersonville High was concerned. "The Outside," therefore, is a reproach to those who saw her struggling and refused to let her in.

She wasn't completely friendless, however. In her first week at school, she bonded with Abigail Anderson (now Abigail Anderson Berard, since her wedding in October 2022). Abigail swam competitively, wanted to be a journalist, and, in Taylor, found an equally aspiring but misunderstood friend. The friendship has been lifelong; in 2017, Taylor was a bridesmaid at Abigail's first wedding, and wrote "Fifteen" about her, compassionately addressing Abigail's misery when a ninth-grade relationship didn't work out. (It appeared on *Fearless*; released as a single in 2009, it was certified double platinum in 2014, denoting 2 million sales. A re-recorded "Taylor's Version" of the track was released in April 2021.) She told CMT Radio: "We were in ninth grade, and singing about that absolutely gets me every time."

It's unsurprising that it makes her cry. It's one of Swift's most personal songs, mentioning Abigail by name and featuring her in the video. (For her role in it, Abigail got a credit as "Taylor's Best Friend" in the film database IMDb.) The lyric documents their first meeting, when Taylor sat next to a red-haired girl named Abigail in class and immediately hit it off with her, and even mentions their mutual dislike of the school cool girls. Abigail's desolation when her boyfriend left her is in the song, too.

To Abigail herself, it's an intensely meaningful song. Although her heart was broken by this boy, a mutual friend of theirs named Trevor, she eventually reconciled with him and they resumed their friendship. A few years after they split up, when feelings still ran high, Trevor included her in a photo book he made for a high school project, pasting three digital pictures of himself and Abigail on a page titled My First Girlfriend. The young couple, posing in a wildflower meadow, look smitten. Alongside, though, Trevor simply noted that they had started dating as freshmen and weren't together long: "I broke up with her."

In the months following their split, Abigail told the *San Francisco Bee* in 2023, she tormented herself with questions: "Why today? Why not yesterday? Is it me?" Tragically, he died in a base-jumping accident in 2016; only then did she learn he had been processing his own trauma. "Regardless of how many people you've dated, there's always that one person that made an impact. And Trevor was my impact," she said, reflecting that "Fifteen" absolutely captures the feel of the relationship that turns out to be pivotal.

Swift was working on material for *Fearless* when she wrote "Fifteen," but before adding it to the album tracklist, she asked Abigail for permission to publicly release it. The song was both about and for Abigail, so she had the final say, and Swift emphasized that if she was uncomfortable about her romantic life being sung about, it was fine and the song would remain their own private tune. Abigail didn't hesitate. She told Taylor she was happy for it to go out into the world; it might even help others who found themselves in the same situation she'd been in. It was just as well that she gave her enthusiastic consent—*Fearless* turned out to be a behemoth: the third biggest-selling album of 2008 in America, where it was eventually certified diamond (10 million copies sold), and winner of the Grammy for Album of the Year, making Taylor the youngest artist to receive the award until Billie Eilish a decade later.

Abigail has 440,000 followers on Instagram, where she posts pictures of holidays, pets, friends from her days at the University of Kansas, and the occasional snap of herself and Taylor. The value both women place on the friendship is summed up by a post from June 2016. It's a photo of a handwritten card from Taylor: "My weird heart loves your weird heart." In the caption, Abigail wrote, "Thank you for getting me. Always."

A sixteen-year-old Taylor performs the national anthem at a Thanksgiving Day football game between the Detroit Lions and the Miami Dolphins. Looking back on the day when she visited Detroit as part of her Eras Tour, Swift reminisced: "I was sooo insanely nervous."

ABOVE: Taylor was a talented singer from a very young age, here singing "The Star-Spangled Banner" ahead of a basketball game, aged just twelve.

BELOW LEFT: Taylor has called her mom, Andrea Finlay, her best friend, crediting her with much of her success. Pictured here at the Country Music Awards in May 2007.

BELOW RIGHT: Taylor with her childhood best friend, Abigail Anderson. Abigail features heavily in "Fifteen" as Taylor tells the story of the ups and downs of teenage love.

ABOVE: Swift discovered she was named after "a guy named James Taylor" after singing "Fire and Rain" at school. By 2011, she was sharing the stage with her namesake, singing the song together at two sold-out shows at Madison Square Garden.

RIGHT: Founder of Big Machine Records Scott Borchetta chose Taylor as his first signing in 2005—but the relationship soured dramatically in 2019 when the company (and Taylor's music) was sold to Scooter Braun. Determined to own her own music, Swift soon began recording her *Taylor's Version* albums.

ABOVE: Swift with the four Grammys she won for *Fearless*: Album of the Year, Best Female Country Vocal Performance, Best Country Song, and Best Country Album.

ABOVE: Swift performing as part of the Fearless Tour. Released in 2008, *Fearless* was to become the most-awarded country music album of all time, earning the singer her first Grammy at just twenty years old.

LEFT: In a now infamous pop culture moment, Kanye West stormed the stage at the 2009 VMAs as Taylor accepted an award for Best Female Video for "You Belong With Me," claiming the award should have gone to Beyoncé's "Single Ladies." West was roundly criticized for the moment, while Taylor has since said she thought the booing crowd was against her.

ABOVE: Taylor with then boyfriend Joe Jonas. Like many of her boyfriends, Jonas is thought to be the subject of numerous Swift songs, particularly featuring on *Fearless* and *Speak Now*, including "Forever & Always," "Mr. Perfectly Fine," and "Better Than Revenge."

RIGHT: *Speak Now* heralded even more awards for Taylor, here at the *Billboard* Music Awards, winning for Top Country Artist, Top *Billboard* 200 Artist, and Top Country Album.

LEFT: Taylor performing on the opening night of the UK leg of her Speak Now Tour. Swift was roundly praised by critics, especially for her showmanship and interactions with her fans.

BELOW: Ed Sheeran and Taylor have developed a close friendship over the years, collaborating on a number of songs, beginning with "Everything Has Changed" in 2012.

RIGHT: The Red Tour was the highest-grossing country music tour of all time, running from March 2013 to June 2014.

BELOW: As her star grew, Swift took the opportunity to sing with another of her icons: this time Tim McGraw, subject of her 2006 hit. Here they are in 2013, performing at the CMA Music Festival.

ABOVE: With *1989* came the birth of Taylor Swift's "Squad," each starring in the music video for "Bad Blood." (*From left to right*): Martha Hunt, Hailee Steinfeld, Cara Delevingne, Selena Gomez, Taylor Swift, Serayah, Lily Aldridge, Gigi Hadid, and Karlie Kloss.

BELOW: The Victoria's Secret Fashion Show was a highlight for musical performers, watched by millions each year. The 2014 show was watched by more than 9 million, and Swift appeared alongside Ed Sheeran, Ariana Grande, and Hozier, singing "Blank Space" and "Style."

Apart from the Abercrombie campaign, the second half of 2004 brought another major step forward. "The Outside," which would appear on *Taylor Swift* in 2006, got its first high-profile public airing and, by extension, got Swift plenty of attention. It was chosen to appear on an album called *Chicks with Attitude*, which was given away free with the purchase of Maybelline makeup. This was a big deal. Teenage "chicks" across America used Maybelline products, so millions would hear her song. It was one of thirteen tracks on the CD; other artists included Swedish alt-poppers The Cardigans and the powerful blues singer Beth Hart. *Chicks with Attitude* was also an eighteen-date summer tour across America, with Liz Phair and The Cardigans headlining. Taylor wasn't on the tour, but she was very much on the album, and told the *Press of Atlantic City* how she found out she'd made the cut. She was eating at a Taco Bell, she said, when Dan Dymtrow called with the news that "The Outside" had been included, and she was overjoyed. She told the paper: "I started screaming. Everybody looked at me like I was crazy."

Like many of her best songs, "The Outside" was written quickly. She was at home on a rainy winter night in 2002, feeling as if her friends had forgotten her, so she picked up her guitar and wrote a song about it. It was pure country-pop, lightly swinging and seasoned with fiddle and acoustic guitar.

Being labeled a Chick with Attitude did her no harm at all, especially since she had the musical craft to back it up. By then, she'd written 100 songs, and it was clear that she was a star in waiting. The next rung of the ladder was about to be climbed.

CHAPTER 4

Paying Her Dues

In October 2004, Taylor had a meeting with Arturo Buenahora Jr., senior director of creative services and production at Sony Music Publishing. Though he had never considered signing such a young writer, when she began to play for him his reservations vanished. "She is a fine, fine songwriter and a good guitar player," he told Hendersonville's local paper, *The Star News*. "If anyone can be that good that early, it's scary how good she will be. Someone like Taylor Swift doesn't walk in your office every day, and when they do, you'd better do your best to work with them." The contract was drawn up on November 1 and signed by Taylor and her parents on January 20, 2005. Once the legalities were taken care of, she was officially a professional songwriter, her main responsibility being the writing of songs she could either record herself or sell to other artists.

An attempt to sell "Teardrops on My Guitar"—co-written with Liz Rose, who would become a significant writing partner—to the Dixie Chicks was unsuccessful, despite Taylor changing the lyric to make it less personal. It had been written about a boy at school who didn't realize Taylor had a crush on him, and his name, Drew, featured throughout. On the demo she recorded for the Chicks, she changed it to "you," but the trio passed on it nonetheless. It was the quintessential blessing in disguise: Swift recorded the song herself, put it on her debut album and released it as her second single in February 2007. Its caressing guitar/mandolin/fiddle arrangement, offset by Taylor's aching vocal, bounced it to No. 2 in the Hot Country Songs chart and also provided her first pop-crossover hit, peaking at 13 in the *Billboard* Hot 100. It won three industry awards, including the BMI Country Awards trophy for Song of the Year. While all of that might still have happened if the Dixie Chicks had bought the song—there would have been nothing stopping Swift from also recording and releasing it herself—their turning it down gave the tune a clear shot at success in its own right, free of associations with any other artist.

A couple of songs *were* bought by others. "This Is Really Happening," co-written with Nashville songwriter Blu Sanders around November 2004, was picked up by Britni Hoover for her album *Country Strong*. Sanders was frankly amazed at his young co-writer's talent. "People like to bash young, successful artists, but Taylor was the real deal," he told *Taylor Swift: The Rise of the Nashville Teen* in 2012.

Australian vocalist Shea Fisher bought an early Swift song, too—"Being with My Baby" (Fisher changed the title to "Bein' with My Baby"). It appeared on her 2009 album *Shea*. By then the song was five years old and Swift was well on her way to global success, but scanning the lyric shows her delicate, poetic touch to have been very much in evidence when it was written. Fireflies, stars, quiet lanes—the picture created by her words quashes any notion that fourteen-year-olds are too young to create meaningful songs. She wrote it with Texas-born songwriter/artist Brett Beavers, whose younger brother Jim, also a successful composer, had a separate writing session with Taylor. Jim's experience with her shows what young writers can be up against.

In 2019, Jim reminisced to Bobby Bones, host of the *Bobbycast* podcast, about their time together. Swift arrived at the writing room at 3:30, driven straight from school by Andrea, who settled herself in another room while Taylor worked. Beavers said he had "learned a great lesson" from writing with her. He was in his thirties, saw himself as a veteran of his craft and had been set up to write with this teenage newbie. "I remember [thinking,] 'What am I doing in a room with a fourteen-year-old girl?'" He assumed they had nothing in common and admitted he arrived with "a bad attitude about the write." Swift soon put him in his place. She already knew what she wanted the song to say, and when Beavers interjected, "Well, you know, an experienced writer like myself might say this [differently]," Taylor was having none of it. Politely but firmly, she told him that what *he* might say wasn't what *she* would say.

Jim's impression of that session was that he had met an artist who knew exactly who she was, what she wanted to express and where she was heading. From that day, those traits—"that vision and focus"—became the first thing he looked for when working with new artists. There was talent everywhere, he said, but artists who connect with the public have something intangible: "They know why they're going to connect." It was almost a sixth sense, coupled with an ability to make listeners feel that the artist is singing directly to them about something meaningful to the artist. There's a sense of kinship with the singer. It can't be taught or bought, which is why some winners of TV talent shows find it hard to keep the momentum going after the initial fizz and firecrackers.

The two had a second writing session but didn't finish the song they were working on. Beavers doesn't even remember its title and blames himself for the collaboration not working out. He felt they weren't meshing—he wasn't "buying into her," as he phrased it—and thought she probably sensed it. And that was that. But there's a postscript. They met again several years later at Sony Publishing's annual Christmas brunch, which is attended by hundreds of employees and songwriters. By then, his young co-writer had become "Taylor Swift," he said, putting figurative quotes around her name. Each year, awards are given to the writer and the artist/songwriter judged to have done the most outstanding work in the past twelve months. This particular year, Beavers was named Writer of the Year, and Swift was Artist/Songwriter. They were seated at the same table and exchanged hello-how-are-yous; then Swift went to collect her award. Beavers remembered her speech: "[Sony has] always been my family; you believed in me when nobody else did. I've grown so much—I remember when I started out, I was writing songs with people like *[looks directly at Beavers]* Jim Beavers." She meant it jokingly, and that was how he took it.

By that stage she could laugh about it, but it had been a struggle to be accepted by some members of Nashville's writing community. She was perfectly aware she would have to work harder and turn up more prepared than an older writer. "I knew that being a fourteen-year-old girl, anybody would—understandably—think, 'I'm going to have to write a song for a kid today,'" she told *American Songwriter* in 2011. Covering all bases in advance has always been her forte, so when she went into sessions she'd already done the groundwork. She arrived at each "with ten or fifteen almost-finished songs, or with developed ideas—finished melodies or choruses." She refused to give anyone an excuse to judge her by her age or gender. "I just wanted to make sure that everybody knew I was serious about it." In the privileged position of having a deal with a major publishing company, she was ready to toil as hard as anyone else.

She regarded the sessions almost as apprenticeships, picking up knowledge from everyone she worked with. Everyone, including those who didn't believe in her or who scoffed at her ideas. Even that kind of session was useful, she said, because "you can make a note to self: 'Never do that to someone else.'" She refused to view herself as disadvantaged: if anything, she prided herself on never saying, "I'm entitled, I deserve more respect."

And sometimes, in those early days, she developed a working relationship with someone who just "got" her. When that happened, she produced some of her most striking work. Liz Rose was the first co-writer with whom she had that instinctive bond, which is evident from the writing credits on *Taylor Swift*—of the eleven tracks on the standard edition, Rose's name is on seven. Together they came up with major early hits "Tim McGraw" and "Teardrops on My Guitar" and, later, the smashes "All Too Well," "You Belong With Me," and "White Horse." They won a mutual award—Best Country Song, for "White Horse"—at the 2010 Grammys, and Swift won Best Female Country Vocal Performance for the same tune. (Also at that year's Grammys, she won the Album of the Year category for *Fearless*, the youngest person until then to win the Grammys' most prestigious award, and Best Country Album.)

At first glance, Swift and Texas-born Rose seem an unlikely team: when they met in 2005, Swift was fifteen and Rose was forty-eight, with a daughter Swift's age. She neither played an instrument nor sang—rare for a songwriter—and only began writing at thirty-seven. They came across each other at a Nashville writers' round, an informal gathering in a bar or coffee shop where songwriters play for a small audience. Despite not being a singer, she sang two tunes that night, and Swift liked Rose's material enough to ask if she'd consider a co-write. Rose agreed but wasn't prepared for the breadth of Taylor's abilities. At the end of the first session, Rose left the room wondering why Swift had wanted a co-writer. "She really didn't need me," she told the *Washington Post* in June 2016, on the tenth anniversary.

They developed a routine, meeting once a week after school in Rose's office. (Rose thought of their sessions as Taylor's "after-school job.") Swift would sit at the piano or pick up a guitar and the two discussed ideas. Most, like their first composition "Tim McGraw," were sparked by events in

Swift's everyday life—that one came to her in math class, she told Rose when she arrived one day. She already knew what she wanted to say and that it would be called "Tim McGraw." Rose was dubious: a song called "Tim McGraw"? What would McGraw himself—one of America's most venerated country names—think? She had reason to feel uncertain. She'd co-written "All We Ever Find" for McGraw's triple-platinum 2002 LP *Tim McGraw and the Dancehall Doctors*.

But when Taylor had recorded the song and it was played to McGraw by his booking agent, he didn't just like it, he wanted his wife, Faith Hill, to hear it, too. That said, he was also bemused that a young artist would use his name in a song. He revealed to Apple Music Essentials in 2021: "I thought, 'Have I gotten to that age now where they're singing songs about me? Does that mean I've jumped the shark a bit?'" He had just turned thirty-nine when "Tim McGraw" came out, but it must have been sobering to contemplate the fact that his name was attached to a song by a fourteen-year-old.

Rose learned never to second-guess Swift. Guesting on a 2022 edition of the *Nashville Off the Record* podcast, she recalled the "Tim McGraw" session. "I guarantee you, that girl . . . I'll bet you in that moment [of writing the song] she saw herself walking off the stage and singing that to Tim at an awards show. That is how brilliant she is." Swift was so confident and prolific that Rose saw herself as an "editor" in the partnership rather than a co-writer. She wondered if she was diminishing her contribution, which was as vital as Swift's, but concluded that editing was "really what I do [with her]." Much of their collaboration involved, she told Y Entertainment in 2014, "moving this there and saying, 'Well, what if we said it like this?' I can remember times when I would try and throw out an idea for a new song: 'How about we write this?' And she would just go, 'Yeah, I don't think so. Go and write that with somebody else.'"

Or they might tussle over a single word, as on "You Belong With Me." The song's protagonist yearns for the gorgeous boy next door, who, of course, is dating the most popular girl at school. In the second verse, the main character glumly reveals that it's Tuesday night and she's sitting at home—and Rose homed straight in on "Tuesday." Why not make it Friday or Saturday in order to stress the loneliness of being at home while the person you love is out with his girlfriend? But Swift wouldn't hear of it. It remained Tuesday, and the song did pretty well for itself. It was an award-winning hit, and was also the song that brought her into contact with Kanye West at the 2009 MTV Video Music Awards.

Rose's favorite is their final collaboration, the 2012 track "All Too Well," which is reputed to be about Jake Gyllenhaal. He and Swift dated from October to December 2010, breaking up just before her twenty-first birthday (Gyllenhaal turned thirty six days later, on December 19). Rose and Swift hadn't seen each other in a while because Swift had completely self-written her most recent album, *Speak Now* (2010), as a way of asserting to doubters that she didn't need co-writers. When Rose got a phone call in early 2011, it couldn't have come at a worse time. She had a sinus infection and was simultaneously clearing out her Nashville house as she prepared to move to Dallas. Four movers were loading up a trailer and Rose was overseeing them when Swift rang and asked if she was free that day. She'd been working on a song and really needed Liz's help. Rose handed the movers the keys to her storage unit and drove over to Taylor's place.

Swift was miserable after a bad breakup and had started composing the song on a day when she was "just feeling terrible about what was going on in my personal life," she told *Rolling Stone*. She hadn't written a song in months, and for this constantly active songwriter it was a telling indication of how unhappy she was. She and her band were rehearsing for the Speak Now Tour, and she began to ad lib the words floating in her head. The band began to play along, improvising riffs, and that was the birth of "All Too Well." Taylor went on to flesh it out during the tour, working on it between shows. At times like this, it was an enormous boon to have writing as an outlet; she poured her wronged heart into it, verse after verse. Whoever the heartbreaker was, he had burrowed into her soul, and his indifferent breakup phone call had devastated her.

By the time she finished the song, which she already knew was special, it was verging on ten minutes long and would have to be trimmed if it was to be releasable on the next album, *Red*. Another problem was that it contained the F-word, which ran so counter to her image that it couldn't appear in the song (it was reinstated on the *Taylor's Version* recording in 2021). The problem was, there was meaning in every word of the song, every line, every verse. Swift's flair for descriptive, novelistic writing reached a peak on "All Too Well." It read more like a diary entry or a letter than a song, and it was easy to imagine it as a handwritten letter, angrily thrust into an envelope and mailed to the person who had treated her as if she were disposable. It is full of thoughts and language rarely found in songs: she remembered the guy telling her father self-deprecating stories, she reminded him of the time they'd danced in the darkened kitchen, and she recalled a conversation with an actress she didn't know. There's no way of identifying the actress, but she approached Swift while she was weeping in the bathroom at a party and asked what was wrong. Every word of "All Too Well" rings true, including a delicately venomous dig about her ex's romantic future: Swift predicted that as he aged, his girlfriends wouldn't; each successive one would be young.

The song hits hard; many Swifties rank it as their favorite. At the highly popular UK-wide club night Swiftogeddon, which plays nothing but Taylor songs, the full ten-minute version is, according to the *Guardian*, "the pinnacle of the evening," despite being "a very long song with no obvious drop and no obvious chorus." Experiencing its anguish together, Swifties hug each other and unite in joyous sadness. For what it's worth, in 2022 Gyllenhaal told *Esquire* that he'd never listened to *Red*—whether that was the original release or *Taylor's Version*, he didn't specify. But he did address the fact that the re-recorded "All Too Well" made him the subject of Swiftie wrath, with so many fans leaving derisory remarks that he turned off comments on Instagram. "It [the Swiftie response] has nothing to do with me. It's about her relationship with her fans," he said, adding that artists have "a responsibility" to ensure that supporters are civil and empathetic, even when they feel the artist has been unfairly treated by another.

Back in early 2011, sitting in the studio with her way-too-long track, Swift knew she needed another pair of ears. That was when she called Liz Rose. Arriving with her notebook, Rose let Swift talk, writing down what she thought were the most pertinent aspects of the breakup story. Taylor gave her "a lot of information" and sang the song, and Rose set about trimming it. She remembered it as being anywhere between ten and twenty minutes long and told the *Dallas Observer* that she'd helped Swift "whittle it down and work on the brilliant pieces of it."

It was time well spent. "All Too Well" was the first track Swift wrote for *Red* and has become one of the most acclaimed of her career, with *Rolling Stone* citing it as "a masterpiece of the breakup ballad form." When the full ten-minute "Taylor's Version" materialized in 2021, it received even greater praise, with *Variety* wishing she would "write another twenty verses and make a full album of it."

Thus, the early collaborations set up for her by Sony Publishing bore quite a bit of fruit, bar the occasional personality clash. The only box that remained unticked was the one marked Record Deal—the holy grail. She'd moved to Nashville, been in development, got a publishing deal and was the youngest professional songwriter on Music Row. Having done the preparation, she was more than ready to move to signed-artist status, which was the only way, in the years before self-releasing music became common, that she would get real traction. She needed a record company behind her to exert itself on her behalf, or she'd remain a low-tier artist competing with a thousand others.

Looking back at the early years during a 2015 interview with *GQ*, she revealed that she'd had a kind of plan B. If the move to Nashville had never taken place and she hadn't become a professional musician, she would have continued to write songs but her focus would have changed. She'd have attended college and afterward gone into a profession like marketing—"a form of business where words and ideas are at the forefront." But it hadn't come to that. Back in 2004, tirelessly working toward becoming a signed artist, she was reassured by the fact that her career was proceeding steadily, if slowly, toward a recording contract. She had the other necessary building blocks in the bag—the publishing deal, the former development deal—so the day she signed her name to a label contract had to be around the corner, right?

CHAPTER 5

Getting Signed

It had to be, and it was. An early co-writer, Robert Ellis Orrall, had been hugely impressed by Taylor's talent and set up a showcase at the Bluebird Café, a ninety-seat room with a sound that especially flattered acoustic music. Improbably located in a strip mall several miles outside the center of Nashville, its setting belies its importance to country music. The *Washington Post* has called it "a sacred space," and it was depicted as such in the hit 2010s TV series *Nashville*. Like the 1970s New York punk club CBGB, the Bluebird is tiny, jammed to capacity, and influential far beyond its size. Vince Gill, Keith Urban, and Lady Antebellum (known since 2020 as Lady A) played early shows there, and Taylor was about to become another artist who eventually would be able to thank the Bluebird for making the stars align.

The place has a tradition of in-the-round performances, meaning the musicians play in a space at the center of the room, surrounded by the audience. Orrall arranged Taylor's invitation-only show for November 4, 2004, at 9 p.m. In the weeks preceding, he and the Swifts left copies of Taylor's press kit at labels all over town. The kit, filled with newspaper articles and a headshot, wasn't homemade, but it had a charmingly homegrown look: it was housed in a clear document envelope with her name, surrounded by silver hearts and stars, pasted onto purple paper. It looked, perhaps deliberately, as if Taylor herself had constructed it in her bedroom. Although she often felt stymied by her age, sometimes it was no bad thing to remind the industry that she was a fresh new talent, unjaded by music-biz hard knocks.

Label interest was piqued and A&R staff from many of the majors turned up for the show. At least one photo from that night exists. The place is packed and there's no stage. Swift is seated on a wooden chair, guitar at hand; additional guitarist Michael Peterson is a couple of feet away; and Orrall is to her left, in front of a microphone. A third musician, Aaron Brotherton, is out of shot. Behind Orrall are his parents, who had come from Boston to see this gig their son had arranged. Andrea Swift is seated at a table against the back wall, her benign expression concealing what must have been considerable nerves, given the importance of the showcase.

But it's the most unobtrusive figure in the photo who is about to assume the greatest importance in Taylor's professional life. He's at the bottom left of the shot, back to the camera, head resting on hand as if to say, "Get on with it." It's Scott Borchetta, who will shortly be offering Taylor a recording contract. He'd been a promotions manager at DreamWorks Nashville, which merged with Universal Music Group in 2003.

Having enjoyed a good deal of freedom at DreamWorks, where he had been encouraged to learn the publicity and A&R aspects of the job, after the UMG takeover, he found himself confined to his promotions job. Increasingly unhappy, he eventually told UMG Nashville chairman Luke Lewis that he no longer felt challenged. Lewis tried to persuade him to stay, but Borchetta was already gone, at least in his mind.

What Borchetta wanted was his own record company, run his way. He began writing a prospectus, which he called "my master's thesis"—it eventually ran to 120 pages, laying out his vision for a new label and explaining why investors might want to come aboard. He took it seriously enough to have top-level meetings about financing. He was still at Universal at this point but his label plan was complete—he'd be free to go ahead in September 2005, when he had seen out his contract.

In October 2004, Dan Dymtrow had sent Borchetta a package containing Taylor's music and press kit. Dymtrow phoned to ask what Borchetta thought, and he replied, "I think it's pretty good." Dymtrow and Taylor were planning a round of label meetings the following Tuesday, November 2, and wanted to see Borchetta. He put them in the schedule for 7 p.m., when everyone else in the office would be gone—no need for anyone at Universal to know he'd planned a meeting with an artist he thought might be ideal for his new company. Which, by the way, he would call Big Machine Records, though he only divulged the name to Taylor after she decided to sign with him. "Big Machine" was a song by American hard rockers Velvet Revolver, and the name appealed to him because, despite the new label not yet even existing, it would announce his presence in a swaggering way. "It's bold and it's disruptive and it doesn't sound corporate," he told *Billboard*. It was also jokey, he said, because the label would be anything but a big machine when it started out.

His reaction to Swift when they met the following Tuesday? "I was just smitten. She was a fascinating person, even at fourteen years old. She had such an amazing desire for people to like her and get to know her." It's hard to sum up why some artists are what's known as "the total package," but Borchetta believed he'd found it in Swift. He took notes during the 2004 meeting and still had them in 2016, when he was interviewed again by *Billboard* on the tenth anniversary of *Taylor Swift*'s release. He read them out to the interviewer. Here's a sample: "This could be your Mick Jagger . . . Taylor takes Japan . . . cover of *Rolling Stone*, host *Saturday Night Live*." His prescience during that meeting was almost on par with Brian Epstein's when he caught a lunchtime pop show at a tiny Liverpool club in November 1961 and decided that this new band, The Beatles, had something about them . . .

"I've been around this my entire life, so when you see that special thing . . . my job is trying to help people achieve their full potential, and she had so much raw talent that [she was potentially] a really big artist," Borchetta told Larry King in September 2016. He almost literally *had* been around outstanding talent all his life. His father, Mike, had been a record promoter for major labels in Los Angeles, and the young Scott got used to the likes of the Beach Boys dropping by the house.

When he appeared on King's show, he could have pointed to the chart performance of *1989* as proof of his astuteness:

that week was its 97th in *Billboard*'s Top 200 album chart. It would spend more than 300 weeks in the chart.

The only problem at the November 2 meeting, which took place in his Universal office, was that Taylor thought Borchetta wanted to sign her to Universal. Obviously, she was beside herself with excitement. Signed to one of Nashville's powerhouses! A week later, he met Scott and Andrea and laid things on the line. If Taylor wanted to sign with Universal, Borchetta would introduce her to the A&R department and the label's other executives. The only catch was that he wouldn't be there. "I'm leaving to start my own label; I don't know what I'm going to call it, I don't have investors yet, I don't know who'll distribute it," he recalled saying in a 2011 video interview. "But I promise you one thing. If you wait, I promise you a record deal. They looked at me like I was crazy [and] said goodbye."

Ten days later, Taylor herself phoned. "I just want you to know that I've made up my mind, and I'm waiting for you." She had been swayed by Borchetta's excitement about her music but also by knowing that she would be the primary focus of attention on his small label. Still tied to Universal for the next ten months, Borchetta was immensely grateful for her faith in him. But shortly after their conversation, his "awesome" bosses at Universal, Luke Lewis and James Stroud, gave him a break. They would keep him under contract until September 2005, but he'd be free to leave six months earlier, in March, to get Big Machine underway.

When Borchetta initially shopped his label idea around to prospective investors, there had been no shortage of enthusiasm, but when he followed up in March he found it difficult to convert promises to hard cash. To supplement what he could raise from them, he put his own money in, as did country star Toby Keith.

According to *Forbes* in 2013, Keith, one of country's biggest names, invested $400,000 for a stake amounting to around 10 percent, as well as setting up a "sister company," Show Dog, which shared staff and office space with Big Machine. The two labels went their separate ways in early 2006, but Keith retained his investment. In 2016, he told the *Chicago Tribune* that he could live on his share of the royalties Swift generated for Big Machine for the rest of his life. "No question . . . A bunch of people could live off that," he said. Scott Swift also bought a stake in Borchetta's venture. According to *Music Business Worldwide*, he paid $500,416.66 on January 1, 2006, for 916,666 common and preferred shares in the company. It amounted to 3 percent of Big Machine's value.

Singers Jack Ingram and Danielle Peck were the first artists actually signed to the label—Ingram's single "Wherever You Are" gave Big Machine its first No. 1 in 2007—but it was Swift whom Borchetta expected to make the biggest splash. In 2011, he recounted the reactions of people in the industry when he introduced them to her. Invariably, he said, they looked as if they were thinking, "So, this is your future? You have this fifteen-year-old female country artist, huh? Way to go, Scott!" The skepticism only fueled his determination.

Back at the Bluebird Café on November 4, though, Borchetta was only one of many intrigued parties. The audience was full of A&Rs who'd received the press kit, and the atmosphere was charged. Taylor Swift, aged fourteen years and eleven months, seemed to be on the verge of something significant. The first four days of November had seen a burst of activity that signaled her star was finally, indubitably, on the rise. The Sony publishing contract had been drafted on November 1 (the Swifts would sign it on January 20, 2005), the meeting with Borchetta took place on November 2, and two days later the Bluebird showcase gave the industry, many of whom had never seen her perform, a primer in what she could do in a live setting. Borchetta, especially, was paying attention. Though he'd been "smitten" at their meeting, he was looking for confirmation that Swift was an assertive live performer.

The night's setlist was brief: "Writing Songs About You," "Me and Britany," and "Beautiful Eyes." Only the last has ever been released, on a 2008 EP of the same name. The first two date back to her early songwriting days, and Swift has recorded both, but they remain in the Vault. Swifties hope that Taylor's Versions will eventually be made, especially for "Writing Songs About You," which was in the running for inclusion on the debut album. Co-written with Sarah Buxton and Victoria Shaw, it streamed for a while on Buxton's MySpace but is not currently online. The lyric is classic Swiftian heartbreak, telling a boy that until she gets over him, she'll write songs about him. She wants to hate him but he's making it impossible—how can she hate him when he looks so beautiful every time she sees him?

Meanwhile, a demo-quality version of "Me and Britany" (frequently misspelled online as "Me and Britney") is on YouTube; for a song reputedly written when she was twelve, it deftly captures the fierceness of friendship between girls— the closeness that impels best friends to spend every spare moment together, then talk for hours on the phone later. The track is as stripped down as it's possible to be, featuring only Swift's vocal and her acoustic guitar. Her voice wavers at times, recounting the closeness they shared: lemonade on the front steps, midnight phone calls when one of them needed to talk and knew there was only one person who would understand, and feeling jealous of a boy who came between them.

Some Swift fans believe that the dreamlike "Seven," from 2020's *Folklore*, is also about Britany. The song's adult narrator flashes back to the year she and her best friend were seven and discovering a world of Pennsylvania creeks and countryside and the simple love that exists between kids who've met their counterpart. Militating against that theory is the narrator's admission that she can no longer picture her friend's face.

Britany was Taylor's Pennsylvania friend Britany Maack, who's remained close to Swift over the decades. How close? In 2016, Swift revealed at Maack's wedding to Ben LaManna, their mutual schoolfriend, that Britany had been "my partner in crime at Brownies sleepaway camp, and she was my date to the Grammys." Swift was maid of honor at the ceremony, the first time she'd been a member of a wedding party. That week saw a typical-for-Taylor juxtaposition of career and personal life: the wedding, which was held in Reading, Pennsylvania, was on February 20, five days prior Swift had been in Los Angeles, accepting the Grammy award for Album of the Year for *1989*.

Back on that night at the Bluebird, the three songs couldn't have taken longer than twenty minutes to perform, but they provided bounteous evidence that Taylor could, as the venue's Erika Wollam Nichols put it in 2019, "actually work a room."

Nichols is now the Bluebird's chief operating officer, but in 2005 she was a waitress, on duty the night Swift played. "Scott [Borchetta] could tell [the songs] were going to hold up in time," she told *People*. Not only that, Taylor was unfazed by playing with three older musicians. She was fourteen but had the unflappability of an adult, which could plausibly be ascribed to having songwriting as an outlet: if she found a situation challenging, she was able to address it by writing about it.

She spotted Borchetta in the crowd, listening with closed eyes. "He was listening better than anyone in the room," she said later, and that was almost certainly true. When he met her parents a week later, he'd made up his mind about her abilities and offered a deal that spelled out his belief in her. The crux was that she would be allowed to write her own songs on every album. There would be no requirement to use other writers' songs—an absolutely critical point for Taylor, who had left the RCA development deal because, among other things, the label wanted her to record cover versions.

In *Journey to Fearless*, she condensed the story of meeting Borchetta into one sentence: "He came up to me after the show and said, 'I want you on my record label, and I want you to write all your own music.'" Later, he confessed that he didn't have an office or a name for the label—"he just had a dream," she laughed.

A couple of days after the Bluebird, Taylor sat down with her diary to try to make sense of everything that was happening. "This last week was CRAZY," she wrote. Capitol Records had expressed interest but weren't offering the deal she wanted; the label felt she wasn't quite ready. Ready for what, she doesn't say, but it didn't matter. "So on the other hand there's Scott Borchetta, who we met with at Universal." She liked him because he'd been passionate about what she was doing, making Taylor feel they were on exactly the same page. "I think that's the way we're gonna go," she wrote, and before ending the diary entry with her "autograph" signature, she reflected that not signing with Capitol was for the best because she didn't want "to be lost on a big label" as she had been with RCA.

"Lost" was the last thing she would be.

CHAPTER 6

Taylor Swift

In a way, the following year, 2005, didn't properly get underway until September 1. Big Machine officially launched that day, and Taylor, now fifteen, was finally a signed artist. (Not for nothing had she started a MySpace account the day before.) But until the company began producing hits—which it would by the end of the year, with Jack Ingram's "Wherever You Are"—it was best known for its link to Toby Keith.

Nashville station WSMV 4 made that clear midway through 2005, when it sent reporter Terry Bulger to Hendersonville High to conduct an interview with Swift in the school cafeteria. As she played a soaring version of "Teardrops on My Guitar," Bulger explained that she had moved to Nashville in the hope of finding someone who liked her music. "Toby Keith did. So much so that he just signed her to his new record label," he said, not entirely accurately. Swift attested to his charisma: "You're in the room with him and you can feel it. There's a power there and you're just like, 'Oh, my God.' I don't think I'll ever get to a point where I won't see him and be like, 'Oh my God, that's Toby Keith!'" (Keith died on February 5, 2024, after a two-year battle with cancer.)

As 2005 went on, she and her parents parted ways with her manager, Dan Dymtrow. It wasn't an amicable split; Dymtrow later sued, claiming they breached their contract by not paying him all the commission he said was owed to him. In 2011, a judge found against all Dymtrow's claims except one: "unjust enrichment." According to the *New Yorker*, the case was settled out of court.

After July 2005, a new day-to-day manager was appointed: Rick Barker, who had looked after Big Machine's West Coast operation. He said something that became ingrained in Taylor's psyche and affected the way she would promote *Taylor Swift* when it was released the following year. He said that if she wanted to sell 500,000 records, she had to meet an equal number of people. In other words, connecting with fans and making them feel they were special to her was of the utmost importance. "He was the first one to ever say that to me, and it sank in," she told *Pollstar*. After that, she would spend up to four hours meeting fans after a show, not leaving until the last person had gotten their autograph and selfie. In 2008, with incessant touring taking a toll on his family life, Barker resigned, but he remained on good terms with the Swifts.

In 2014, he modestly told *Pollstar* that he took no credit for Taylor's success. "She told me, 'I want to be the biggest star in the world.'" Her strategy was to go out and meet as many people as she possibly could." Meeting her fans became second nature, but she found it hard to comprehend her elevated status—the idea that meeting her could make someone's day. Talking to CMT after *Taylor Swift*'s release, she was still bemused: "People line up and want me to sign things. I still haven't been able to grasp the fact that if I sign a piece of paper, it might mean something to somebody."

The main work of 2005, though, was putting together *Taylor Swift*. Her choice of producer was Nathan Chapman, a Nashville native who had produced a few demos for her. He hadn't expected to have a career in music—though he played guitar and had written songs, his life's aim was to be an English professor. But while studying in France for a summer, he met his wife-to-be, Stephanie Schlosser, an aspiring singer-songwriter; back in Nashville, he got session work as a banjo and mandolin player, while Stephanie landed a publishing deal with Jody Williams Music and began writing songs with Liz Rose. Rose, of course, happened to be working with another aspiring songwriter: Taylor Swift.

Stephanie's publisher heard demos that Nathan recorded for her, was "blown away," and Chapman was consequently asked to produce a few demos for Taylor. The songs he worked on, which included "Our Song," "Picture to Burn," and "Tim McGraw," turned out exactly as she'd hoped—and she was a demanding artist, so that's saying something. "I know exactly where I want the hook to be . . . what instruments I want to use," she said shortly before album sessions got underway.

Jody Williams sang Chapman's praises to *The Tennessean*: "He has a natural relational ability with any creative person he meets. There's this instant, 'Let's cut through all this other stuff and make music.'" That's why, when Taylor began to record the album—the start date was November 3, 2005, according to Robert Ellis Orrall, who would produce several of its tracks—she tried out several people for the position of main producer but kept returning to Chapman. She described him to CMT as "this demo producer who worked in a little shed behind this publishing company [Sony] I was at."

The other producers Big Machine tried pairing her with were "awesome," she said, but the songs she made with them didn't have the warmth and fullness—"the magic," as she put it—of Chapman's tracks. (His own voice can be heard on some tracks on the finished album; it's detectable as a low, gentle accompaniment to her own vocal.) Not only that, he "got" exactly what she wanted to do. As mentioned above, she wrote songs with a fully formed idea of how they should sound: where the mandolin would come in, how the drums should sound, how low in the mix the bass would be. With Chapman, all that was needed was a ten-minute conversation, "and he brings it all to life," she told CMT News. Her ideas were so fleshed out even at the demo stage that the demos ended up sounding very close to what eventually appeared on the album.

Big Machine were still cautious because Chapman was new to album production, but Scott Borchetta finally gave in: "OK, try some sides with Nathan." Chapman knew about Scott's hesitance—on Bobby Bones's *Bobbycast* podcast, he remembered a speakerphone call from Taylor and Borchetta, who asked him "to go in and track some songs." Chapman was aware that it amounted to an audition, because Scott wasn't sure Taylor had made the right choice. "[He was thinking,] '*This* guy? The demo guy?'" Chapman told Bones with some amusement.

But Swift had made up her mind. Chapman recalled: "I was twenty-eight, she was fourteen or fifteen and neither of us had a clue what we were doing. I certainly didn't have a clue what was going on. I was just making songs." Because both were feeling their way along and neither had a professional reputation to worry about, they could be honest with each other. If Chapman thought her voice wasn't up to scratch that day, he would say so and tell her to go home, and she was equally candid—he remembered her saying, "Dude, that track is horrible!"

Ultimately, they gelled because each, in their way, was an outlier. "She was writing these songs that were super-oddball for the time—[for instance] 'Tim McGraw' was the title of one of the songs!—and they didn't fit anywhere," while he was doing arrangements and production that were "pop with country instruments" rather than anything that could be identified as traditional country music. "To Scott's credit, he gave me a budget. He gave the demo guy a budget."

In the end he produced every track on the standard edition of *Taylor Swift* (which Swift herself often refers to as *Self-Titled*) except "The Outside," which was co-produced with Orrall. The latter also produced several songs on the deluxe and bonus editions.

Swift and Chapman were such a productive pair that he was the only producer, other than Swift herself, on her second and third albums, *Fearless* and *Speak Now*, and he was credited on eight of the sixteen tracks on the standard edition of fourth album *Red*. He worked on just one track on the next, *1989*— the record that reframed her as a pop artist—and didn't contribute to any subsequent records, but there were no hard feelings. "She didn't fire me, she just changed genres," he told Bobby Bones in 2022.

She spent around four months recording the debut and viewed the result as a diary brought to musical life. Heard as a complete album, it's an exceptional capture of a sixteen-year-old girl's life: the daily grind of school, the bumpy roads of friendships and love relationships, and the tsunami of emotions that sometimes swamped her. Arguably, the track that best depicts her state of mind is the sometimes overlooked "A Place in This World," written just before she turned fourteen. A gentle mid-tempo song made plaintive by pedal-steel guitar, it spells out the ambivalence of teenage life—she doesn't yet know who she is or what she wants; she feels alone yet self-sufficient, happy yet anxious. Like every teenager in history, she's looking for "a place in this world." The song meant a lot to her. Until she decided that the LP should be self-titled, its working title was A Place in This World, and she was "really happy [that the track] is on the album, because I feel like I finally figured it out."

Now her fear of "running out of time" if she'd stayed in development at RCA made sense. If she'd waited till she was eighteen, the debut would have been another record entirely. She'd known back then that the poetry in her head would have been lost—there would have been no "Teardrops on My Guitar," "Picture to Burn," or "Tim McGraw."

Especially no "Tim McGraw," which Big Machine decided would be her first single. Taylor was taken aback. She thought the song was great, but it didn't strike her as the one capable of introducing her to the world. Borchetta was insistent. "Tim McGraw" (which was originally called "When You Think Tim

McGraw") had to be the one. She was a new singer, virtually unknown outside Nashville—so debuting with a song called "Tim McGraw" would be incredibly canny, because it would force the question: "Who's this girl singing about Tim McGraw?" (Side note: in May 2012, Borchetta signed McGraw himself to Big Machine, by then a busy and flourishing label.)

The release of "Tim McGraw" was set for June 19, 2006. This was the test: would Taylor grab record buyers and the all-important radio programmers? The photo used on the sleeve couldn't have been more country, and it was also true to the song. Taylor, wearing a yellow sundress and holding a posy of small yellow flowers, is leaning against the front bumper of a vintage pickup truck—perhaps a Chevy, as named in the song— and the squared-off toe of one of her cowboy boots is just visible. (The 7-inch vinyl version, still shrink-wrapped, was for sale on eBay for $600 as this book was being written.)

Big Machine's new office on 16th Avenue South, where it's still located today, was then almost unfurnished, and the company had only around ten staff members. The paint on the walls was still wet. On March 10, 2006, a full three months before release day, Taylor, Andrea, and Chapman came in to help mail out the CD single to radio (the copies aimed at radio stations contained the album version and a slightly shorter radio edit). "We sat out on the floor and did it because there wasn't furniture at the label yet," Taylor recalled to *Entertainment Weekly* in 2008, by which time not only was the office furnished, it could also point to *Taylor Swift* as a huge success and confidently predict that the follow-up, *Fearless*, to be released later in 2008, would be equally barnstorming.

But in 2006, Taylor couldn't know what would happen, and with every CD she dropped into a padded yellow envelope, she said a prayer that the recipient would listen to it—liking it would be a bonus. Radio staff received dozens of promo submissions every week, so it wasn't a given that her song would even make it onto the office CD player, let alone be aired at a playlist meeting.

Big Machine had been working to ensure the single would receive a warm welcome. Its campaign received an invaluable helping hand from the influential cable TV channel Great American Country (since renamed Great American Family), which made Swift the subject of a twenty-one-minute documentary titled *A Place in This World*. It aired on May 8, nudging her name and face into the consciousness of viewers a few weeks before the single came out. It was screened again on October 22 to promote the release of *Taylor Swift*.

As introductions to new artists go, the documentary is textbook-perfect. Swift's natural ebullience is given free rein—she screams as she hugs a friend, laughs in disbelief as she thinks about making her red-carpet debut at the Academy of Country Music Awards, punches the air remembering the first time she heard "Tim McGraw" on the radio ("I almost drove off the road").

But those teen-girl glimpses are balanced by legend-building footage of her playing the Grand Ole Opry, posing for photographers at an event, and playing a new song for friends as they sit around a campfire. Her friends' rapt expressions speak volumes about the gap that was opening between them and Swift. Though she scrupulously maintained her friendships—

and to this day is still close to high school friends like Abigail Anderson—it was impossible to pretend that she wasn't changing or that her classmates still regarded her as "just Taylor." Her dream, she tells the camera, "is to look out into a crowd of thousands of people and have them singing the words to my songs. That to me would just be everything I've ever hoped for."

"Tim McGraw" duly made its appearance on June 19. It took its time to reach the main singles chart, finally docking at No. 86 on *Billboard*'s Hot 100 on September 23, but it made a much quicker impression on the Hot Country Songs list—on July 1, it was No. 60. Its eventual highest position was No. 40 on the Hot 100 and 6 on Hot Country. The country chart used a complicated system of measuring "listener audience for each spin a song received" to tally a record's position. That meant, in the case of "Tim McGraw," that audiences loved the song.

Its fortunes were also helped along by its video, which premiered on Great American Country on July 22. By then, GAC considered Swift enough of a sure thing to turn the first showing into a big deal, sending out a press release to announce that it would debut at 2:30 p.m. and for the next ten days would only be available to watch on GAC.

Though the single was also reviewed positively in the press, most of the reviews didn't run until after *Taylor Swift* came out on October 24. PopMatters mentioned it in its article about the debut album: "A suitably twangy and atmospheric, mid-paced ballad, 'Tim McGraw' is good enough to recall some of the best country singles of recent years." CMT News gave it an unconditional thumbs-up: "It is easily the most sensuous and catchy coming-of-age song since 'Strawberry Wine,'" a

1996 single by country vocalist Deana Carter. Some reviews appeared even later still, such as *Rolling Stone*'s salute in 2020, praising the "majesty" of Swift's "writerly sensibilities" and declaring it the eleventh best debut single of all time (it was denied a place in the Top 10 by The Smiths' "Hand in Glove").

Taylor had just finished tenth grade at Hendersonville High when the single came out. That would be her last year at a conventional school; her career commitments were mounting—one of them being a forthcoming six-month radio station tour—and attending class every day was no longer feasible. The answer was home-schooling, and she enrolled at Aaron Academy, a private institution in Gallatin, Tennessee, that offered accredited home-learning from kindergarten through to twelfth grade. The school's mission, posted on its website, is "to assist and encourage parents who are training and educating their children and to help these students achieve the highest academic standards in Christian education." Taylor would complete eleventh and twelfth grades via Aaron's program, studying while on the road, in airports, and in hotel rooms after shows. She was quick and adept, finishing her junior and senior years in a single year. Theoretically, that made her eligible to receive her diploma in 2007, but it arrived (by mail) in July 2008 instead. She told the Associated Press: "Education has always been at the forefront of my priorities, so I'm really glad to have my diploma."

Graduating wasn't her only academic achievement. Fourteen years later, there was another—one she hadn't expected. On May 18, 2022, she became a Doctor of Fine Arts, thanks to an honorary degree conferred by New York University. Dr. Swift, as she now was, attended the commencement ceremony at Yankee Stadium in cap and gown—the first time she'd ever worn the traditional graduation ensemble. She posted a clip on Instagram that showed her dressing for the event, four-inch leopard-patterned heels and all. Later, she addressed the graduating class with easygoing wit and brio—no surprise there, because by that point speaking to crowds in stadiums was second nature. "Hi, I'm Taylor. Last time I was in a stadium this size I was dancing in heels and wearing a glittery leotard. This outfit is much more comfortable."

Her speech eloquently touched on her life and how her experiences might be applied to the graduates' own lives: "Part of growing up . . . is about catch and release . . . knowing what things to keep and what things to release. You can't carry all things, all grudges, all updates on your ex, all enviable promotions your school bully got. Secondly, learn to live alongside 'cringe.' Cringe is unavoidable over a lifetime. I'm a big advocate for not hiding your enthusiasm for things. It seems to me that there is a false stigma around eagerness. Never be ashamed of trying. Effortlessness is a myth."

There was more, every word couched in big-sisterly optimism—at thirty-two she was a decade older than many in her audience—and hope for the future. She concluded: "We will breathe in . . . breathe out. And I am a doctor now, so I know how breathing works. We're doing this together. So let's just keep dancing like we're the Class of '22." It's hard to imagine anyone in the crowd not being at least a little charmed. And if it wasn't the first commencement speech ever included on the song-lyrics site Genius, it must have been very nearly the first. As is customary on Genius, users even highlighted and explained parts of the speech. In the passage about "living with cringe," for instance, she recalled spending the entirety of 2012 dressing like "a 1950s housewife." In a helpful annotation, a user explained that she had worn vintage dresses throughout the *Red* album era. Another user chimed in: "This also could've been an Easter egg for the first track off her tenth album, *Midnights*, entitled 'Lavender Haze.'" (More on Easter eggs at the end of this chapter.)

Back in 2006, after finishing tenth grade, she went straight into an intense promotional period. "Tim McGraw" was beginning to do well, the album was on its way and her job now was to criss-cross the country, playing shows and dropping in at radio stations. She appeared at the July 22 Aquapalooza and consciously stepped up her MySpace posts. As previously mentioned, no country artist had recognized the potential of social media until Swift made it a significant part of her promo toolkit. She had always responded to as many fans as she could on the site but now she redoubled her efforts and in each reply mentioned that her debut album would be out soon. According to Scott Borchetta, it was the triple barrage of her online presence, *A Place in This World*, and the "Tim McGraw" video that won over radio. Big Machine was able to approach country radio and point out Taylor's growing stature as an artist—she was still a minnow, but thanks to her efforts, which were tireless, she was starting to create a small ripple in the ocean.

Taylor needed the extra lift-off because radio station research showed that listeners weren't enthusiastic about "Tim McGraw." The stations based their findings on several metrics, including listener surveys and tracking sites that show what stations are playing, and the word was that the song wasn't landing. That was especially true of older male listeners. It was deeply disappointing news; in the days before streaming, radio was the medium that introduced new artists to the millions listening at home or in their cars. Despite her popularity on MySpace, which was increasing by the day, if she wasn't on the radio, she wouldn't go much further.

The reason Big Machine's radio pluggers tenaciously stuck with it—apart from the fact that the MySpace and *A Place in This World* activity were having an impact, making their task easier—was that they knew country radio was desperate for younger listeners. Having a permanent place in the hearts of its traditional over-thirty-five demographic wouldn't stop stations from atrophying if they didn't start lining up a younger audience to eventually take the older generation's place. For the past decade, promoters of rock festivals have openly fretted that there are few obvious young successors to festival-headlining titans such as Coldplay—and country radio was in much the same position around 2006.

The pluggers knew it, and Borchetta and Rick Barker knew it. So when some stations refused to playlist "Tim McGraw" because it didn't perform well in their research, Taylor made a direct appeal to fans on MySpace. She wrote: "I'd like to thank whatever station you're hearing my song on," and fans quickly fed back information about where they were hearing it. Barker and the label went to stations that had given it a few spins but hadn't pushed it hard because of the negative market research. Those stations were informed that the research must be wrong, because people were messaging Taylor on MySpace, saying they had heard the single on that particular station and loved it. So while the research said one thing, actual listener feedback sent a completely unambiguous message: "Station XYZ played 'Tim McGraw,' and I'll keep listening to XYZ as long as they keep playing it."

Seizing the moment, Taylor and Andrea went on a nationwide radio tour. Hearing the word "tour," Taylor expected a tour bus, but no—there was a rental car, Andrea at the wheel and almost enough space in the back seat for Taylor to take a nap. She was known to arrive at stations with a batch of home-baked cookies; there's footage of her at Nashville's WSIX, a plastic bowl of invitingly gooey chocolate-chip morsels sitting on a countertop alongside a paper plate with a handwritten message: "Taylor Swift x. Homemade cookies. Eat."

They visited station after station, and at each Taylor played a few songs, generally in the conference room, with a couple of DJs as her audience. She also conducted phone-ins with fans, leaving each caller dazzled; the definition of a "people person," Swift is never more herself than when speaking to fans. Actually meeting her and being subjected to the double whammy of her charm and her talent changed programmers' minds. If Swift had a maxim, it would be this comment, from her 2020 documentary *Miss Americana*: "I'm only here because I work hard and I'm nice to people." It certainly worked this time: "Tim McGraw" crept onto playlists. And just as the radio tour ended, she joined country trio Rascal Flatts as their opening act on the last nine dates—from October 19 to November 3—of their Me and My Gang arena tour.

She had only two days' notice that she would be joining Flatts, because until their Madison Square Garden show on October 14, the opening act had been Eric Church. The self-described "loud, rowdy" country rocker considered himself and Flatts a "horrible match" and seemingly went out of his way to express his sentiments by consistently playing too long. He was fired after overrunning by twenty minutes at the Garden.

"And Taylor called, 'cause she's great, and said, 'Hey, I don't want there to be any bad blood here between us,'" Church told *Esquire* in 2023. "I said, 'Nah, it's great—they're gonna love you. Only request I have is, your first gold album—I want it.'" And he got it. As soon as *Taylor Swift* went gold, in February 2007, she presented a gold disc to him "on a [tour] bus somewhere" on which she had written: "To Eric, thanks for playing too loud and too long on the Flatts tour. I SINCERELY appreciate it." Greatly tickled, he later donated it to the Country Music Hall of Fame.

When she received a phone call on October 17, 2006, telling her she was replacing Church, she "screamed louder than I can ever remember screaming before," she confided to her diary. At the top of that entry, which was dated October 18, she wrote: "OH MY GOD I am on the RASCAL FLATTS TOUR." Just above that, she had noted: "Mediabase: 14 Billboard: 17"— the slots then occupied by "Tim McGraw" on *Billboard*'s country chart plus the country chart compiled by radio-monitoring service Mediabase.

Halfway through the tour, on October 24, *Taylor Swift* was released. Conveniently, Flatts were on a five-day break between shows in Fairborn, Ohio, and Austin, Texas, and Swift was able to promote the album and track her sales. In the first week, it sold 39,000 copies, and, reportedly, she was mildly disappointed, assuming that would be its highest weekly sale. No: it climbed the next week, and every week thereafter. After Rascal Flatts, she toured as George Strait's support act from January to March 2007, with Brad Paisley from April to November, and with Tim McGraw and Faith Hill in July, during a break from Paisley's tour. She was also booked to open for Kenny Chesney, but a few weeks later, before she joined his tour, she was dropped. It was sponsored by a beer company, and at seventeen, she was four years too young to be involved.

In all, she opened fifty-nine shows in that twelve-month period, and for every twenty-five-minute set she played, she acquired 15,000 new fans—or at least 15,000 people who would remember her the next time they heard "Tim McGraw" on the radio. No wonder she looks back on it so fondly, saying years later: "I loved it. Those were some of my favorite times."

As per Rick Barker's advice to "meet 500,000 people," she spent hours after every show signing autographs and posing for pictures. At the same time, sales of the debut were rising, week after week. She hadn't expected that—and if she'd been able to look into the future, she would have been even more astonished to see that *Taylor Swift* wouldn't mark its biggest single-week sale until January 5, 2008, fourteen months after its release. It was purchased 187,000 times that week, and they were "pure sales"—meaning the album had sold that many copies, either physically or by download, as opposed to simply being streamed. Swift thought it was deeply odd that, instead of showing the album steadily dropping down the chart, every weekly report revealed higher sales. It took some time before she joined the dots between that and her after-show autograph sessions. She had done it herself: simply by meeting fans and showing gratitude for their support, she recruited thousands of people to Team Swift, and many of them—now known as Swifties—would still be there for the Eras Tour fifteen years later.

Most of the initial reviews were in the country press, though her home-state daily paper, the *Philadelphia Inquirer*, also found room for an assessment of *Taylor Swift* and gave it a thumbs-up. "Her slightly husky voice balances between open-hearted innocence and life-scarred experience," it observed, and praised the songs' lack of "bubblegum angst or melodrama." *Country Weekly* said it was "preoccupied with the concerns of a teenage girl, for sure, but demonstrating an honesty, intelligence, and idealism," and the *Palm Beach Post* gave it an A for being a "contagious" evocation of "teenage angst."

In years to come, a flurry of "serious" reviews of *Taylor Swift* would emerge; once it was clear she was truly a singular songwriter and was in it for the long haul, publications that hadn't necessarily seen her as a lasting artist in 2006 reappraised her and published thoughtful essays about the debut. *Billboard*, for instance, asserted in 2017 that it was the best of all her albums; it was Swift "in miniature," and her future self and importance to pop was already asserted by this record and its vulnerable, detailed songs. Pitchfork's 2019 review also found that "her detailed lyrics and canny worldview were there from the start." It poked friendly fun at Swift's southern drawl on "Picture to Burn"—an accent that had long disappeared by 2019. AllMusic's 2016 piece, meanwhile, spoke admiringly of her use of Tim McGraw's name as "a marker in a lover's timeline"—many songs about romantic breakups contain similar references to people and places, but here it was deployed as a hook, and "manages to come off as an original idea."

Despite admitting to CMT in December 2006 that the album made it seem as if she'd "had 500 boyfriends"—which wasn't the case, she hastily added in case someone thought it was true—she was deeply proud of what she'd created. Part of her validation came in the form of conversations with other teenage girls. At a 2007 solo acoustic set at the Revival bar in Ontario, she told the audience she was constantly approached at shows by girls who told her that listening to *Taylor Swift* made them feel as if she'd torn pages out of their own diaries. "And hearing something like that really makes me feel like I've done something good. It makes me realize I've done what I'd wanted to do. Which is ultimately [to] make people feel like they're not alone."

Around the time of the Revival show, she found time to make a Christmas EP, *The Taylor Swift Holiday Collection*, which came out October 14, 2007. It comprised four covers and two originals—"Christmas Must Be Something More," which had an openly Christian message, and "Christmases When You Were Mine," a classic lonely-this-Christmas ballad. At a time when she was busy writing for *Fearless* and touring with Brad Paisley, it filled the album-shaped gap that had been created by the lack of new material since *Taylor Swift*. Her only Christmas collection to date, it had sold 1 million copies by 2019.

Four singles followed "Tim McGraw." "Teardrops on My Guitar" was released on February 20, 2007; "Our Song" on

September 10; "Picture to Burn" on February 3, 2008; and "Should've Said No" on May 19, 2008. (Note: The original version of "Picture to Burn," which appeared on the standard edition of the debut, provoked comments about its use of the word "gay." It was in the first verse, and the song's context didn't make it clear whether it was used factually or as an insult. The line was changed on a radio remix and for the album's deluxe edition.)

"Should've Said No," which unofficially closed the *Taylor Swift* era, emerged as she was in the middle of making *Fearless*, and it would have been excusable if her mind had been elsewhere. But it wasn't. Blessed with a gift for multitasking, her mind was right there, intent on doing her best for "Should've Said No." *Country Weekly* singled it out as one of *Taylor Swift*'s best songs, and that was borne out by its chart performance: though it only got as far as No. 33 in *Billboard*'s Hot 100, it topped the Hot Country Songs chart—her second Hot Country No. 1 after "Our Song."

Infused with banjo and fiddle yet as propulsive as a pop song, "Should've Said No" trod similar bad-boyfriend ground to many of the debut's tracks, but it was angrier in its delivery. The *Chicago Tribune* deemed it a "revenge song," and as such it resonated with many listeners. And Swift's performance of it at the Academy of Country Music Awards in May 2008 emphasized the "revenge" element. She started the song wearing jeans and a hoodie with the hood up, almost obscuring her face—a most un-Swiftian outfit. Strumming her guitar, she sounded almost sullen, as if the boy in the song was a bad one indeed. Ninety seconds into the song her outfit is torn off, revealing a black dress, and she sings the rest of the tune as if getting a load of anger off her chest. It was a strong performance—strong enough to be released as the official video for the single.

If *Taylor Swift* was about a real girl and her life, it also shared one of her quirks: a love of hidden messages. She played around with the lyric booklet, encoding each lyric with a message, and a week before the album's release she wrote a MySpace post to let fans know: "All the letters of the songs are lowercase, except for random capitalized letters. Put them all together, and you might find out some hidden messages about the song."

It was the start of a tradition beloved of Swifties and Swift herself. Later, the coded lyrics were superseded by Easter eggs—clues hidden in everything from videos to onstage props to the color of her clothes. The obscurer the better: an example is a red scarf worn in a short film directed by Swift and released in November 2021 to accompany "All Too Well (Taylor's Version)"—the ten-minute take of the song, which had been in the Vault since she wrote it for *Red*. Swifties identified it as representing Taylor's virginity, but whether they were right or way off the mark is a mystery; Swift never explains Easter eggs.

The debut's coded messages were:

"Tim McGraw" "Can't tell me nothin'"

"Picture to Burn" "Date nice boys"

"Teardrops on My Guitar" "He will never know"

"A Place in This World" "I found it"

"Cold As You" "Time to let go"

"The Outside" "You are not alone"

"Tied Together with a Smile" "You are loved"

"Stay Beautiful" "Shake 'n' bake" (This is probably a reference to a favorite film of hers, *Talladega Nights*, in which it's used as a catchphrase.)

"Should've Said No" "Sam Sam Sam Sam Sam" (Sam was a high school boyfriend who supposedly two-timed Taylor.)

"Mary's Song (Oh My My My)" "Sometimes love is forever"

"Our Song" "Live in love"

Every single went platinum (1 million sales) or multi-platinum, and the album sold 7 million copies in the US alone. As of August 2023, it had spent 280 nonconsecutive weeks in the *Billboard* album chart. It also got her a 2008 Grammy nomination for Best New Artist. She lost to Amy Winehouse, but any disappointment would soon be assuaged. A whole mantelpiece's-worth of Grammys and countless other awards were coming her way.

CHAPTER 7

Fearless

Yo, Taylor. I'm really happy for you, I'mma let you finish, but Beyoncé had one of the best videos of all time! One of the best videos of all time!"

Kanye West shrugged and exited the stage, an astonished and speechless Swift staring after him. It was September 13, 2009, she had just won the MTV Video Music Award for Best Female Video for "You Belong With Me" and, thanks to West suddenly interrupting her acceptance speech, everyone in America now knew her name. As for Beyoncé, whose "Single Ladies (Put a Ring on It)" had been nominated in the same category, she was as stunned as Swift, mouthing, "Oh, Kanye!" as she watched from the audience.

Swift had already made history that night by being the first country singer to win a VMA. Now, she was famous as the artist whose thunder was stolen by Kanye West. It even brought her to the attention of President Obama, who called West "a jackass." Backstage, Swift told reporters: "I was really excited because Kanye West was onstage. Then I wasn't so excited anymore after that. I don't know him and I don't want to start anything."

If the encounter made her a household name, she'd been heading that way anyway, thanks to *Fearless*. Released on November 11, 2008—"You Belong With Me" was its third single—it was a transitional record. *Taylor Swift* had made her a country star; *Fearless* made her a country-pop star, with the emphasis on "pop." AllMusic even called it "one of the best mainstream pop albums of 2008"—a bold assertion in a year that also saw the release of Lady Gaga's *The Fame* and Beyoncé's *I Am . . . Sasha Fierce*.

Commerce-wise, too, *Fearless* made the music industry take notice. *Forbes* reported in January 2009 that, thanks to the combined sales of *Fearless* and *Taylor Swift*, Taylor was 2008's biggest selling artist. *Fearless* had only been available for the last seven weeks of 2008, making her feat doubly impressive— between the two records, she racked up 4 million sales. Had the debut not kept selling throughout 2008 and her sales were calculated by *Fearless*'s performance alone, Taylor would have ended up in second place to Lil Wayne, whose *Tha Carter III* shifted 2.9 million copies that year. But the following year, *Fearless* was the unchallenged champion, with another 3.2 million sales in 2009. Adding *Taylor Swift*'s 2009 sales to that figure brings her total to 4.6 million albums bought in a store or downloaded. Perhaps that's why the highly influential Country Music Association named her Entertainer of the Year at its 2009 awards ceremony—the youngest person ever to win its flagship award.

She'd arrived at the 2009 VMAs in a horse-drawn glass "princess" coach, from which she emerged wearing a full-length glittering silver dress. If anything ever signaled that she was now living a fairytale, this was it. She was still Taylor, still giving a voice to the preoccupations of teenage girls—yet she had undeniably moved on. The first single from *Fearless*, "Love Story"—which turned into a mind-bendingly huge hit; by 2015, it had sold 8 million copies in the US—said as much. If the boy she loved would just run away with her, she would magically become a princess. And here she *was*, a real-life princess, or at least dressed like one. She still thought of herself as a country singer, albeit one who was "lucky enough to have [songs] played on pop radio," as she told the *Oakland Press*, but her life was different now.

In real life, she never dated the "Love Story" boy, much though she wanted to, because her family disliked him—thought he was "a creep," in fact. The star-crossed situation of would-be lovers kept apart by others reminded her of *Romeo and Juliet*, and the idea evolved into "Love Story." In the video, she carried the idea further by dressing as Juliet alongside singer/model Justin Gaston, playing Romeo, also in costume. Though their look was more nineteenth-century Regency England than fourteenth-century Verona, they made a convincingly lovelorn couple. Meanwhile, the song itself was wildly catchy, appealing as much to pop fans as to country lovers. Released on September 15, 2008, it sold and sold. With such a huge single under its belt, *Fearless* followed the sales path of "Love Story" when it was released two months later, setting the trajectory that would gradually turn Swift from successful country artist to pop phenomenon.

It's important to add that she was careful to assure fans that, despite appearances, she *wasn't* a princess. On "White Horse," the second single from *Fearless*, the chorus even spells it out. In the storyline, she's facing the idea of being alone after she's been let down by the boy she loves, but mingled with the heartbreak is determination, even optimism. She knows she can go it alone, and by the end, she's deriving strength from refusing to return to him. In the chorus, she tells herself she's *not* this boy's princess and *isn't* living in a fairytale. That can also be taken as a message to fans. "White Horse" came out on December 8, 2008, almost exactly nine months before she would win that Best Female Video MTV award. It was as if the track was saying: in a few months, you might see me turning up at awards ceremonies in a glass coach pulled by a pair of white horses, but trust me: that shimmeringly beautiful young woman will still be me.

Nevertheless, Swift's songwriting on *Fearless* undeniably tilted toward fairytales and fanciful subjects. She admitted as much to CMT News: "I am completely fascinated by the differences and comparisons between real life and fairytales because we're raised as little girls to think that we're a princess and that Prince Charming is going to sweep us off our feet." While writing for *Fearless*, she even came up with a tune called "Today Was a Fairytale." (It didn't make the album, but eighteen months later, when she was cast in her first movie, the 2010 rom-com *Valentine's Day*, she released it as a single and saw it climb to No. 2 in the US and No. 1 in Canada. Swift played a high schooler who's going out with her classmate, played by seventeen-year-old Taylor Lautner. In real life the two did date from around September to December 2009, and he would be the subject of a *Speak Now* song, "Back to December.")

Yet of all the songs on *Fearless*, the one that most moved her was one completely unrelated to make-believe. The dreamy ballad "Fifteen," inspired by her friend Abigail's relationship heartbreak, was difficult for Taylor to sing—she felt Abigail's pain so keenly that she cried in the recording studio. We know this because the album's hidden messages include this one for "Fifteen": "I CRIED WHILE RECORDING THIS."

One of the reasons *Fearless*'s first single, "Love Story," set her on the road to mainstream stardom was its sound. It was less country than her first-era singles: the mandolins and dobros were less pronounced, while the guitars and drums were more prominent in the mix. That could well have been Swift's idea. She was now co-producing alongside Nathan Chapman, and it was clear that her interests were taking her in a different direction from *Taylor Swift*.

She began writing *Fearless* while opening for Brad Paisley in the spring of 2007. Arriving at a venue early, she often had time to kill and would closet herself in an empty room—frequently a locker room—backstage. The first significant song she wrote, the one that determined the direction of the rest of the LP, was the title track. Early in the process, she decided that she was going to avoid writing about her current reality, which was hotel rooms and tour buses. "I got albums when I was younger and there would be songs about that sort of thing, and I couldn't really relate to it," she told the *Oakland Press*. So, when the idea for "Fearless" bubbled up in her consciousness, she instantly saw its potential. "This is a song about the fearlessness of falling in love," she explained on the Big Machine website. It was a love song, but written with nobody special in mind—she was single, traveling from city to city, and "wasn't even in the beginning stages of dating anybody." In the absence of a boyfriend, she'd recently found herself thinking about first dates, and from there she wondered what a first date could be. "So, this song is about the best first date I haven't had yet."

From there, she delved into her inner life, imagining her next relationship but also observing her friends' relationships. In that sense, she was like any sixteen-year-old girl, fascinated by the dramas swirling around her small suburban town. Thus, for example, were "White Horse" and "You Belong With Me" created. Both would come to be seen—along with "Love Story" and "Fifteen"—as cornerstones of *Fearless*; they were the fan favorites, released as singles along with the title track. Her plan had been to save "White Horse" for the third album, but the producers of her favorite show, *Grey's Anatomy*, wanted to use the track in the first episode of Season 5, on September 25, 2008. (She loved the series so much that she named one of her beloved cats Meredith Grey, after a character in it. Another was Olivia Benson, after the star character of *Law & Order: SVU*, and the third became Benjamin Button, as in the Brad Pitt movie.) An overjoyed Swift was left with no choice but to add the song to *Fearless*, and when the show aired, she filmed her reaction: watching with a group of friends, she jumped up and down, hugged herself, and said it was "one of the best moments of my life."

Landing a song on *Grey's Anatomy*? Yes, things were very different now. One marked difference was that from here, the boys who inspired her songs would be cut from a different cloth. Though *Fearless*'s songs were still about boys she knew from school or had met in Nashville, she was coming into contact with actors and big-name musicians now—guys she would never have otherwise encountered. In the summer of 2008, halfway through recording the album, Swift played a few shows with the Jonas Brothers, then at their heartthrobby peak with their first No. I album, *A Little Bit Longer*. She and middle brother Joe, four months her senior, dated between July and October, splitting shortly before *Fearless* was released. Interviewed on Ellen DeGeneres's chat show soon after the record came out, Swift was open about her disappointment that Jonas had ended the relationship. "There's one [song on *Fearless*] that's about that guy," she said, glancing at a photo of Jonas and herself projected on Ellen's video screen. "That guy's not in my life anymore, unfortunately. That's ouch."

DeGeneres pointed out that while she might not have the guy, she could at least write a song about it. "*Yes!* I got a last-minute recording session, right when [the relationship was ending]. My label let me record that song ["Forever & Always"] right before the album had to be done." She was finding it hard to forget him, she went on, not least because she saw his picture on T-shirts everywhere she went. She ended the chat with Ellen on a hopeful note, though. She knew she would meet the right person, and when she did, "I'm not even going to be able to remember the boy who broke up with me over the phone in twenty-five seconds when I was eighteen."

Fast-forward eleven years: by 2019 she and Jonas had made up and become friends, and his relationship with Camilla Belle, the actress for whom he left Taylor, had long since ended.

Appearing on *Ellen* in May 2019, she said she regretted "putting [Jonas] on blast on your [2008] show. That was too much."

"Forever & Always" was one of the most vituperative tunes she'd ever written. A country-rocker that turns into a guitar-heavy arena-rocker halfway through—the forcefulness of the electric guitars compels her to shout over them, furious in her misery and picking holes in everything Jonas said during their three-month fling. He told her he loved her but then stopped calling; he promised to be there forever and always but now makes her feel like a stranger; she apparently said she loved him, too, but it scared him into running away. Though the finished album was imminently due to be handed to Big Machine, Swift insisted that "Forever & Always" be added to the tracklisting. It was never released as a single, but it still clocked up 1 million sales and streaming units by 2018. Joe Jonas, by the way, put on a good show of not minding the song. Interviewed by *Seventeen* in June 2009, he said: "It's flattering. It's always nice to hear their side of the story."

The intimacy of her writing—in which, for instance, her reimagining of *Romeo and Juliet* could feel like the chronicle of a real romance—would make *Fearless* the go-to album for sensitive, romantic girls. That was helped along by Swift's own approachability. At a time when many of the biggest female pop stars were either actresses playing pop stars (such as Miley Cyrus's portrayal of Hannah Montana) or sexualized fodder for gossip websites like TMZ (e.g., Britney Spears and Christina Aguilera), Swift was a safe space for teenage girls.

Not only was she decidedly not a rebellious teenager, she actively wanted to be a role model. "I'm constantly face-to-face with people who are buying my music; I look them in the eye every single night. And I hear it all the time . . . where a mother would come up to me and say, 'Thank you for being a role model,'" she told the *Pasadena Star-News* in January 2008, just after being voted Superstar of Tomorrow at the Young Hollywood Awards. "I never, ever want to let those people down. I let that govern my life, and I'm proud of it. I do what I can to live right and to set an example. I consider myself lucky to be in this position."

Of the thirteen songs on *Fearless*'s standard edition, Swift wrote seven alone ("Fifteen," "Love Story," "Hey Stephen," "You're Not Sorry," "Forever & Always," "The Best Day," and "Change"); four with Liz Rose ("Fearless," "White Horse," "You Belong With Me," and "Tell Me Why"—the first was also co-written by Hillary Lindsey); one with country singer John Rich ("The Way I Loved You"); and one with singer-songwriter Colbie Caillat ("Breathe," which features the two women harmonizing sumptuously). She was moving toward total ownership of the songwriting process and would achieve it on the next album, *Speak Now*, on which she wrote every song alone.

On release, *Fearless* went straight to No. 1 on the *Billboard* chart—the first of eleven nonconsecutive weeks at the top. Notably, during the second of those weeks, the entire Top 3 was composed of women who might have been deemed pop rivals, with Britney Spears's *Circus* at No. 2 and *I Am . . . Sasha Fierce* by Beyoncé at No. 3.

Reviews were generally positive. Rock critic Robert Christgau was "moved" by *Fearless* being, in effect, a "concept album" by an "impossibly strong and gifted teenage girl"; *Blender* declared that she had "the personality and poise to make these songs hit as hard as gems like 'Tim McGraw' and 'Our Song' from her smash debut." The *Guardian* was sparing in its praise, deeming it "a record that does something bland and uninventive but does it incredibly well," but concluded that Swift's success in the UK—*Fearless* was her first major release in Britain—was more or less guaranteed: "You occasionally find yourself wondering if the world really needs any more music like this. The feeling that the world is going to answer your query in the affirmative swiftly overwhelms you." Ten years later, Kaitlyn Blythe reassessed *Fearless* for the Australian site Junkee and found that it had lost none of its power. It "feels like being a teenage girl felt . . . It has the sparkling hope of a young woman thrilled to finally be stepping into adulthood."

With *Fearless* a roaring success, it was past time for a headlining tour of her own. Swift had deliberately waited till she was confident she could fill arenas—the kind of venues she had played as opening act to Paisley, Strait, and the rest. "I never wanted to go into an arena and have to downsize it," she said, and whether she knew it or not, her attitude put her in a category of her own. It's vanishingly rare for an artist to play arenas on their first headline tour—even the biggest boy band of the 2010s, One Direction, settled for 4,000-capacity theater venues before graduating to bigger rooms.

On the 118-date Fearless Tour, which launched on April 23, 2009, at the Roberts Municipal Stadium in Evansville, Indiana, only one of the tour stops was in a theater. It was her pair of gigs at London's Shepherd's Bush Empire, one of which was reviewed by the *Guardian*. The reviewer noted that Swift was accustomed to much bigger venues in America but put on a great gig even without the snazzy stage set used at her other shows. "It probably helps that her milieu is country-pop, a genre based on the principle that the show must go on, but it's still impressive how enthusiastically she gets stuck in."

The stage set *was* impressive because no expense had been spared. There was a castle, winding staircases, six dancers, seven musicians, eight costume changes, five guitars—and 150 personnel behind the scenes, charged with getting the tour from place to place. By the time it wrapped up at the Gillette Stadium in Foxborough, Massachusetts, on June 5, 2010, Swift had played to 1,207,887 people and grossed $66,246,496. Great news for all involved, but Swift was probably just as delighted with the reviews: the *Hollywood Reporter* named her "country's new queen," while the *Los Angeles Times* took a different view of her genre but was just as enthusiastic: "When she stood beneath a cascading waterfall to close her encore, she looked every bit the pop star." MTV singled out her practice of walking through the crowd, hugging as many fans as she could, but her core strength was perhaps best defined by the *Phoenix New Times*: "In the end of the pre-show video, Swift defined 'fearless' as 'going out onstage and giving it your all every night.' Indeed."

When Taylor began her *Taylor's Version* re-recording project, she started not with the first album but with *Fearless*. Working on it between November 2020 and February 2021, she was, in effect, doing an experiment. Should she impose changes on beloved songs? How had the intervening twelve years affected her feelings toward them? Would anyone pay to hear reworkings of such cherished tracks? "You Belong With Me," "Love Story," "Fifteen"—these were canonical, perfect as they were. She would soon find out whether she'd done the right thing.

"When I think bAck on the fearless album and all that you turned it into, a completely involuntary smile creeps across my face. This was the musical era in which so many . . . hands touched, so many unbreakable bonds formed . . ." she wrote on social media on February 11, 2021. The capital *A* in the fourth word was part of a hidden message that spelled APRIL NINTH, which turned out to be the album's release date. She'd stopped encoding messages after the *1989* album, switching instead to Easter eggs, but returned to codes for the *Taylor's Version* records.

Back in August 2019, she'd announced on *Good Morning America*: "My contract says that, starting November 2020, I can record albums one through five all over again," and now she had come up with the goods. The four re-recordings made available so far have stayed more or less faithful to the originals; the big difference is her vocals, which have matured over the years and are less girlish and breathy.

Never mind the small matter of *Fearless* being album two; she would soon explain that. In an interview released on February 12, 2021, by Republic Records, the label she signed to after her Big Machine contract expired in 2018, she said: "Deciding on what album to re-record first was pretty easy for me. I always gravitated toward *Fearless* because I think that, as an album, it was a real coming-of-age. And I look back on that album and it fills me with such pride, and it was an album about hope, and lessons learned, and the effervescence of teenage youth and all that. What more fun than to go back and explore that?"

Fearless (Taylor's Version) also fulfilled hopes commercially. It debuted at No. 1 in the US and was the country's fifth best-selling album of 2021; in the UK it also hit No. 1, as it did in several other countries. Once again, Swift had listened to her instincts and been proven right.

CHAPTER 8

Speak Now

Swift being Swift, she used the downtime on the Fearless Tour to write the next album, *Speak Now*, which would be released on October 25, 2010. "Writing" meant writing every song herself—the first time she'd crafted a record without co-writers. Swift was adamant that it had to be her name and hers alone listed in the credits because, as she recalled to *Rolling Stone* in 2019: "When I was eighteen, they were like, 'She doesn't really write those songs.' So my third album I wrote by myself as a reaction to that."

At the same time, simple expedience often dictated her working methods. Though she started writing in the summer of 2008, she did the bulk of it in 2009–10 while touring *Fearless*. She was often alone when an idea popped into her head—in the middle of the night after a show in the Midwest, say. Rather than writing half the song and putting it aside until she could get together with a co-writer, she simply finished it there and then. It happened again and again, and she came to realize that she could do the entire record on her own. That doesn't mean she didn't work with any other writers—she did, but none of those songs made it onto the album. She and Nathan Chapman, who was back on co-production duty alongside Swift, had a saying: may the best song win. To date, *Speak Now* is her only entirely self-written LP.

The album turned out to be transitional in its themes. She worked on it at the end of the 2000s, and there was something of a new-decade feel to her change of focus. It was still a country longplayer, albeit with a sliver of pop in the grooves, but she was no longer writing about teen romance. She was still a teenager a few months from her twentieth birthday when she began work, but her boyfriends were no longer Hendersonville High swains with pickup trucks. The "boys" she met now had careers and had lived a bit—as had she. Yet *Speak Now* also stuck to a few of the old ways: it was co-produced by Nathan Chapman and recorded almost entirely in Nashville.

The dawning feeling of independence was heightened in the spring of 2010 by a move into a condo in the center of Nashville. It was her first home of her own, the idea of which delighted her. Newly installed in the 3,240-square-foot apartment, she told interviewers of her excitement at having her own closets, her own dresser drawers—the tiny things that, taken together, meant she was in charge of her own domestic life. Among other modern conveniences, the apartment had a spiral staircase ascending to a birdcage/tree house, and in the living room was a pond—lily pads and koi carp included. The look she was going for, she said during a Ustream live chat on July 20, 2010, was "a pirate ship slash *Alice in Wonderland* slash an old antique store slash a fortune teller's house slash a tree house slash a birdcage slash a garden slash a very mismatched place."

The gentle, acoustic *Speak Now* song "Never Grow Up," written after she spent her first night in the apartment, addressed her ambivalence about being an adult. Excited as she was about having her own space, there was a bittersweetness about leaving the security of her family; the song examined the simple perfection of her childhood versus her young-adult desire for independence.

The album's original title was *Enchanted*, after a song of the same name. The track was thought to have been inspired by Adam Young, the one-man music project who records under the name Owl City. That was the conclusion reached by fans, who found the name ADAM embedded in the "Enchanted" lyric, and further credence was given to that interpretation when Owl City covered the song. As ever, Swift has never publicly revealed who inspired the song, but she did tell the *Our Country* blog: "It was about this guy that I met in New York City, and I had talked to him on email or something before. And meeting him, it was this overwhelming feeling of: I really hope that you're not in love with somebody." The apparently mutual infatuation didn't develop into a relationship, but Young was bowled over by her gesture and released his cover version on Valentine's Day 2011, no less. Through the years, the song remained a favorite of Taylor's, to the extent that it was the only *Speak Now* song performed on the Eras Tour until "Long Live" was added three months in.

Enchanted remained the working title until Scott Borchetta, having heard the entire album, pointed out that it didn't suit the songs. The new record wasn't about high school romances—she'd experienced much more life since the last full-length, and her writing had changed accordingly. Within minutes, she decided it would be called *Speak Now*, after the song of that name, which was written after she'd had a heart-to-heart with a friend. The friend's ex-boyfriend was marrying another woman, and the phrase traditionally spoken at weddings—"speak now or forever hold your peace"—came to Swift's mind. She felt it applied to her own situation too, inasmuch as she had the choice of either speaking through her songs or remaining silent, never expressing herself. Swifties have debated ever since whether the friend who inspired the song was Paramore singer Hayley Williams; the two were, and remain, close friends.

The words "speak now" also fit the album's concept. "I've experienced a lot of things that I've been dying to write about and a lot of things that I wanted to say in the moment that I didn't," she said during a Ustream chat. New people had come into her life in the past two years, she went on, and she sometimes regretted not telling them exactly what she was thinking. "This album is my opportunity to do that. Track by track, each song is a different confession to a different person." In the album's written "prologue" (liner notes), she urged fans to express themselves, too: "There is a time for silence. But if you . . . clearly know what you need to say, you'll know it. I don't think you should wait. I think you should speak now."

"Confession" usually implies that the confessor is apologetic or remorseful, making it the wrong word for some of these songs. There *is* a song with that specific intention—the wistful, rock-leaning "Back to December," which marked a first for her, insofar as she'd never said sorry to someone in a song. "This is about a person who was incredible to me . . . and I was really careless with him," she told *E! News*. She didn't share the poor guy's identity, though in a way she did. The hidden message in the lyric was TAY, which seemed to point to Taylor Lautner. Once their relationship was behind them, they became friends, and he appeared in the video for "I Can See You," a track resurrected from the vault for *Speak Now (Taylor's Version)*. "He was a very positive force in my life when I was making the [original] *Speak Now* album," she said in 2023. (Improbably, when Lautner married in November 2022, it was to yet another Taylor—a registered nurse named Taylor Dome.)

The other tracks, however, weren't confessions. "Mean," which would win Best Country Song and Best Country Solo Performance at the 2012 Grammy Awards, was anything but confessional. It addressed critics who claimed she was a weak singer and was said to be based on a particularly sniping critique by industry analyst Bob Lefsetz. He targeted her appearance at the 2010 Grammys, where she picked up four awards (Album of the Year, Best Country Album, Best Country Song, and Best Female Country Vocal Performance). At the ceremony, she sang "Rhiannon" with the song's author, Stevie Nicks, and—there's no sugarcoating this—she was off-key. Although Lefsetz admitted that *Fearless* deserved its AOTY trophy, he homed in on the live performance.

"How awful was she? Dreadful," he wrote, then expanded at length about the "awfulness" before predicting that her career would never recover. As any Swiftie could have told him, her career didn't hinge on powerhouse vocals. She was loved for her songwriting, empathy, and what website Slant Magazine called "one-of-us authenticity"—and that kind of connection to fans isn't severed by a bum note in a TV performance. Swift's answer to the criticism was "Mean," the most traditionally country song on *Speak Now*. Traditionally? It was full-fledged country satire: in the video, which is set in a farmyard, she and her band stomp around bales of hay with old-time, banjo-thumping gusto.

"You never really ... get past things hurting you," she told *60 Minutes*. Poignantly, the lyric admits exactly how hurt she was: when critics slate her for her "flaws," all they're doing is telling her something she already knows—that she's not the strongest vocalist on the block. She says exactly that in the song: don't tell me I'm not the best singer because I'm already aware of that. Happily, she had the pleasure of seeing "Mean" embraced as an anti-bullying anthem; meanwhile, she'd be able to point to its pair of Grammy awards—the only Grammys won by *Speak Now*—the next time a critic put down her ability.

"Better Than Revenge," another much-commented-on song, instantly became one of the most controversial tracks she'd written. It was thought to be about losing Joe Jonas to Camilla Belle, and heaped wrath not on Jonas but on Belle. A roaring power-pop song, it angrily accused a rival of swiping her boyfriend; controversy entered the picture in a verse that explicitly shamed the rival's sex life. Many critics took issue with it, deeming the song (and by extension Swift) anti-feminist. Despite Swift declaring herself a feminist, some critics couldn't square that with the insult she flung at the other woman. Even many years later, "Better Than Revenge" was still sometimes cited as proof that she was anti-progressive. In 2023, when recording *Speak Now (Taylor's Version)*, she changed the contentious line, substituting the word "matches" for the original "mattress."

As with nearly everything Swift does, the alteration was debated among Swifties, some of whom felt that it would drive streaming traffic to the original version—a highly undesirable outcome as far as they were concerned because the party that stands to benefit is Shamrock Holdings, which bought the masters to her first six albums in 2020. (More on this in Chapter 13.) Despite the judgmental tone of the line she changed, a number of fans deem the line to be important in a history-preserving sense because it was part of the original work.

Swift was open about "Innocent," a pedal-steel-accented country ballad, being about Kanye West—more than that, it wasn't just *about* him; it directly addressed him. After the VMAs incident, she took her time working through her feelings and came to realize that writing a song would enable her to let it go. "Innocent" extended an olive branch, telling West that his onstage outburst didn't define him—he was an innocent soul. "It doesn't really add anything good if I start victimizing myself and complaining about things," she told *New York* magazine. Swift intended the song as a gesture of care toward an artist who was often volatile, but some considered it misplaced. Slant Magazine was among them, calling it a "patronizing, condescending sermon," but that was balanced by the opinion of country music journalist Chet Flippo: "Sometimes forgiveness is the sweetest revenge, and it's what she achieved."

On September 12, 2010, she got the chance to debut "Innocent" live—at the VMAs, aptly enough. It was almost exactly a year since the ceremony where the beef, as such, began, and Swift did a brief, arresting performance of the song. She didn't perform the song she'd been nominated for in the 2010 awards—"Fifteen," which was up for Best Female Video (the category was won by Lady Gaga's "Bad Romance")—perhaps deciding that singing a track from her new album was a better use of her onstage time than reviving the two-year-old "Fifteen."

"I had a bunch of different options going into the VMAs," she told *Access Hollywood*. "I could've sung a different song, I could've not gone, but I felt like going to the VMAs and singing a song about how I had felt . . . it seemed like the right call if I'm going to live my life in the way that I wrote that album," she said. Barefoot and wearing an unshowy white dress, she sang "Innocent" in front of footage of the previous year's encounter with West. The irony was that West was about to grab all the headlines for the second year running. But this time, it was for his stunning show-closing performance of "Runaway," a track from his upcoming album *My Beautiful Dark Twisted Fantasy*. He got the night's only standing ovation, and when the album appeared on November 22, it was almost universally declared a masterpiece.

The best-known of *Speak Now*'s non-confessional confessions was the country-rock ballad "Dear John." It was widely thought to be about singer-songwriter John Mayer, whom she dated from December 2009 until spring 2010. Mayer himself assumed it was about him, inducing a tart retort from Swift: "How presumptuous! I never disclose who my songs are about." The expression "Dear John" is common parlance for a letter (or nowadays email) written by a woman to end a relationship with a man, so the song could have been about anyone, Swift maintained. Whoever the culprit is, he appears to have greatly hurt her. The song positively seethes. Swift accuses him of taking advantage of her youth (if it was Mayer, he was thirty-two to her nineteen), of offering love then withdrawing it, and of "burning out" many other girls before meeting her.

Before all that, she had appreciated Mayer's music—he had won multiple Grammys, including the 2003 Best Male Pop Vocal Performance citation for "Your Body Is a Wonderland," and was highly regarded for his guitar skills. So Swift looked forward to their first meeting, and it was highly productive: he'd written an Americana-leaning song, "Half of My Heart," and felt that Swift, whom he didn't personally know, would make a good duet partner. In another age, he'd have asked his manager to call her manager to gauge interest. But it was March 2009, so he simply tweeted about it. "I want to sing it with Taylor Swift. She would make a killer 'Nicks' in contrast to my 'Tom' of a song," he wrote, alluding to Stevie Nicks and Tom Petty's duet on the 1981 hit "Stop Draggin' My Heart Around." He followed the tweet with a direct message to Taylor, as he revealed in an iTunes interview: "[I said,] 'I have this song, I think you're the one for it.'"

Swift agreed to do it. After the session, he couldn't praise her highly enough: she had an incredible work ethic, and once she'd committed to doing it, she was determined to stay for the hours and hours it took to perfect the track. Awed, he called her "a tank"—it was a compliment—and contrasted her attitude to that of some other musicians he'd worked with, who he said had "raced" to get the job done. "Half of My Heart" appeared on his November 2009 album *Battle Studies* and was a single, reaching No. 34 in the *Billboard* Hot 100.

Their relationship appeared to have started by December, when they performed the song at the Z100 Jingle Ball at Madison Square Garden. Their microphones were next to each other; there were sidelong glances and Mayer angled himself to face her throughout the song. It was evidently a heady experience for both, rather understandably: Mayer was a rock heartthrob at the time, and Taylor was pure blossomy gorgeousness. When the romance ended a few months later, Swift channeled the pain into "Dear John," which to this day has few competitors in her catalogue when it comes to lighting a fire under an ex-boyfriend. (Again, she has never said the song is about Mayer.) Her gift for storytelling served her well, with zingers in every verse. Her life once "revolved" around the man in the song, but she now sees him as playing a "dark game"—and there's much more vitriol besides.

Mayer was taken unawares by the track, he told *Rolling Stone* in 2012. He felt he hadn't "done anything to deserve it" and was "humiliated" by his lack of foreknowledge, revealing that she hadn't called to let him know it would be on *Speak Now*. The song was held by many critics to be one of her best; Chris Willman of *Our Country* went so far as to call it "her masterpiece to date."

"The Story of Us" was about the same person who featured in "Dear John," she told *USA Today*. Some fans had thought "The Story of Us" was directed at Taylor Lautner, but if Swift's own word wasn't proof enough, there was also the lyric's coded message: CMT. The 2010 CMT Music Awards ceremony was held in Nashville on June 9, and Swift had been nominated for Video of the Year and Female Video of the Year (both for "You Belong With Me") and Collaborative Video of the Year (for "Best Days of Your Life," with Kellie Pickler). She was there, and so was Mayer, who was performing with Keith Urban on an Urban song, "Hit the Ground Running."

Musically, the two songs—"Dear John" and "The Story of Us"—couldn't be more dissimilar: "Dear John" is mournfully country, the other pounding power-pop. What links them is Swift's wounded heart. On which subject, the hidden lyric message in "Dear John" is "Loved you from the very first day," which affords an idea of how much she'd invested in what turned out to be a brief relationship. Perhaps she and the song's subject had different ideas about their situation, with Swift believing there was more to it than he did. It would explain what seemed to be bewilderment on Mayer's part when she came up with "Dear John"—he said he'd learned to be "accountable" for his actions in relationships and thus felt Taylor had dealt him a low blow.

Regarding the possibly Mayer-inspired "The Story of Us," she told *USA Today* that the song was conceived after she and a former boyfriend were seated near each other at an awards ceremony. Neither spoke to the other, and Swift found it agonizing to be in the same room. She was desperate to talk to him—to acknowledge his presence, at the very least—but couldn't bring herself to break through the "silent shields" they'd both erected. When she got home, she told her mother that although the room had been packed, she'd felt as if she were alone. "Then I got up and ran into my bedroom, as she's seen me do many times. And she probably assumed I had come up with a line in the song. And I had."

Note: Swift's 2022 album, the Grammy-winning (in the Album of the Year and Pop Vocal Album categories) *Midnights*, contains what might be a final word about that relationship. The *3am Edition* of the record has a bonus soft-rock track called "Would've, Could've, Should've," co-written with Aaron Dessner, her frequent collaborator since the *Folklore* album. It searingly looks back at a romance with an older man that seemingly still troubles her—but, again, don't assume it's Mayer. She knew every lyric on *Midnights* would be pored over for clues to who inspired each song, but she was exasperated by attempts to pinpoint her "inspiration." She touched on the same subject when *Reputation* came out in 2017, writing in a self-produced magazine that many people assumed her writing process was so simplistic that all she did was compile a list of a recent boyfriend's traits and turn them into a song. As far as she was concerned, that assumption boiled songwriting down to a formulaic recipe as binary as "a paternity test."

"The Story of Us" was the last song she wrote for *Speak Now*. Intuitively, she knew the album was done. That track would become the LP's fourth single in April 2011 (after "Mine," "Back to December," and "Mean," and later joined by "Sparks Fly" and "Ours").

Big Machine prepared for *Speak Now*'s October 25 release by shipping 2 million copies to retail, and not just to conventional record shops. Scott Borchetta, who knew that *Fearless*'s extraordinary success meant everyone would be watching, was relying on the "huge trust factor" that existed between Swift and the Swifties. But he also foresaw a demand at outlets like Starbucks (which had been selling albums since 1994), Rite Aid, and Radio Shack, and his instinct was accurate. By taking the album to where people shopped, he saw it sell 1,047,000 copies in its first week. The only female artist who had ever had a better opening week was Britney Spears, whose *Oops! . . . I Did It Again* sold 1.3 million copies on its first week in 2000. The media began to speak of Taylor as "a pop megastar."

Borchetta predicted that *Speak Now*'s sales would exceed 2 million by the end of 2010, and he was right—it hit 2.96 million. He also thought it had a good shot at being the best-selling record of the entire year, despite coming out in late October. That particular achievement eluded Swift; she had to settle for third biggest after Eminem's *Recovery* (3.4 million) and Lady Antebellum's *Need You Now* (3 million).

The performance of *Speak Now*'s singles confirmed that real superstardom was within her grasp, with all except "The Story of Us" reaching the US Top 20. That last, one of the most out-and-out poppy on the album, stalled at 41, conceivably because core country fans weren't won over.

Striking while the iron was steaming hot, on November 23 Swift announced the Speak Now World Tour. It kept her on the road, excepting occasional breaks, for thirteen months, from February 2011 to March 2012. Grossing $123 million, it was the biggest selling tour by a woman that year—and it goes without saying that, while chalking up these vast numbers, she was already thinking about the next album, *Red*. By the time the Speak Now Tour finished, she'd written an entire album's worth of new material, though only half of those songs would end up on *Red*. It also goes without saying that Swift's productivity and sheer lust for work—her near-superhuman desire to achieve—puts her very nearly in a class of her own.

The North American leg of Speak Now was sponsored by CoverGirl cosmetics, which signed her to an endorsement deal in 2010. The campaign launched in January 2011 and saw her fronting ads for the NatureLuxe range. The products, including NatureLuxe Mousse Mascara, Silk Foundation, and Lip Perfection lipstick, used their lightness and natural origins as their selling point (a "heavy synthetic" was replaced with beeswax, for example) and the fresh, vibrant Swift was the ideal face for the range.

Also in 2011, she struck a deal with cosmetics giant Elizabeth Arden—license-holder for Britney Spears's perfumes—to produce her first fragrance, Wonderstruck. As every Swiftie knew, the name came from a line in "Enchanted" and the bottle approximated the shade of purple Swift wore on the cover of *Speak Now*. Three gold charms—a birdcage, a bird, and a star—dangled from the bottle's neck. It made a pretty package and, at just $21, was within the reach of most teenagers. The scent, described by Beautinow as "fruity-floral with dominant notes of raspberry, apple blossom, and peach," was popular enough to spawn another four fragrances: Wonderstruck Enchanted (2012), Taylor (2013), Taylor Made of Starlight (2014) and Incredible Things (2014). The range was discontinued in the mid-2010s but is often available on eBay; as of this writing, a bottle of the original Wonderstruck, with charms still attached but bottle-top missing, was $699 plus postage.

Tickets for the Speak Now Tour started at $25—a virtual giveaway compared to the huge increases that have become standard in the live-music industry in the 2020s. (The cheapest general admission Eras Tour ticket on the North American dates was a highly reasonable $49, but rose to $499 for VIP packages. Saying that, Swift wasn't to blame for ticketing-industry economics and was charging what the market would bear. VIP packages for Eras" UK leg were sold in different tiers, with the most expensive costing around £662 and including "an unforgettable reserved seated ticket" along with some covetable merchandise: a tote bag, an interactive VIP tour laminate, prints expressly designed for VIP ticketholders and more. There were on-the-night perks too: priority check-in, a separate entrance, and crowd-free merch shopping before the show.)

Speak Now also saw Swift's first move into live albums: *Speak Now World Tour—Live* was designed as a souvenir for people who had been to the shows and as a view of a typical show for people who hadn't. What it couldn't offer to the latter group was the sense of anticipation generated every night by wondering what cover version she would perform in the last third of the set. She changed it every night, and the breadth was remarkable: they included Alanis Morissette's "You Learn," Pras's "Ghetto Supastar," and the first song Ron Cremer taught her, Cheap Trick's "I Want You to Want Me."

Notably, there were very few country covers on *Speak Now,* and those she included were nearly all for the benefit of audiences at her southern and southwestern shows—country's heartland. As an example, her choice for the show at the KFC

Yum! Center in Louisville, Kentucky, was "The Back of Your Hand" by country veteran Dwight Yoakam. Elsewhere, it was rock, pop, and R&B.

At some gigs she was joined by a special guest, and the two would sing one of the guest's songs. It's probably safe to assume that, back in Wyomissing, she had never pictured the day when she would duet with Nicki Minaj on "Super Bass" or with Flo Rida on "Right Round." Note: The Minaj date took place in August 2011. Four years later, the women had an exchange of words on Twitter that changed Swift's understanding of racism in the music business. In July 2015, Minaj was surprised and disappointed that neither her brilliant video for "Anaconda" nor her collaboration with Beyoncé, "Feeling Myself," had been nominated in the MTV Video Music Awards' all-important Video of the Year category. She landed nods in the Collaboration, Hip-Hop, and Female slots, but Video of the Year was the one that mattered because, like the Oscar for Best Picture, it grabbed the lion's share of media coverage.

Minaj jokingly wondered whether she had somehow "missed the [voting] deadline," then wrote a series of tweets that made her point clear. She believed that the contribution and influence of Black women on pop culture was systemically overlooked, and the VOTY snub proved her point. (Beyoncé had in fact been nominated for VOTY with a solo track, "7/11.") Swift, nominated for "Bad Blood," felt Minaj was leveling blame at her. She tweeted: "I've done nothing but love & support you. It's unlike you to pit women against each other. Maybe one of the men took your slot." (Kendrick Lamar, Ed Sheeran, and Mark Ronson/Bruno Mars had also received nominations.)

An exasperated Minaj replied: "Huh? U must not be reading my tweets. Didn't say a word about u. I love u just as much. But u should speak on this." Swift made a misplaced conciliatory gesture: "If I win, please come up with me!! You're invited to any stage I'm ever on." The spat began to attract celebrity input, with Sheeran, Mars, and Katy Perry offering their opinions. Two days later, a chastened Swift responded: "I thought I was being called out. I missed the point, I misunderstood, then misspoke. I'm sorry, Nicki." Minaj gracefully accepted the apology; Swift learned a lesson. Her country background had instilled an aversion to discussing controversial subjects—the reason she had never, as Minaj urged, "spoken on" racism in the music industry—and she now understood more about the intersectionality of misogyny and racism. (At the VMA ceremony, on August 30, 2015, "Anaconda" won the Best Hip-Hop award, and "Bad Blood" Video of the Year.)

Back in 2011, if the array of guest singers on the Speak Now Tour wasn't a hint of where her own music was heading, her fourth album, *Red*, would deliver the message even more bluntly: Swift could have stayed in her country bubble, but for this tirelessly creative and highly ambitious artist, standing still wasn't an option.

CHAPTER 9

Red

She *could* have stuck with what had worked before. That almost happened. Writing in her spare time on the Speak Now Tour, Taylor came up with a batch of songs that she demoed with Nathan Chapman. Scott Borchetta liked them and assumed that was the new album right there, more or less done and dusted. But while demoing, Swift had become dissatisfied, and her response to Borchetta made it plain that her music had to change. In an interview with *Our Country* she recounted what she'd said to Borchetta: "I think it's good, but I don't think it's different enough." This being album four, it was high time to leave her comfort zone and find out what else was out there.

The fact was, she already knew what she wanted to do. It was time to use a "group" approach to make an album. She had been inspired by the experience of collaborating with guest singers while touring *Speak Now*, explaining to *USA Today*: "We had so much fun pulling other artists in and letting their styles rub off on our performances, singing their songs and having it become sort of a duet." She loved the feeling of taking a journey every time a new guest joined her onstage and wanted to recreate the same bold group dynamic on *Red*.

For years, she'd admired Swedish super-producer Max Martin and American master-craftsman Jeff Bhasker. Between them, they'd worked with everyone from Kanye to Britney to Beyoncé to Drake. "There are these songwriters and producers I've admired from afar and been influenced by, but I've never had the courage to sit in a room and make music with them," she told *Parade* magazine in 2012. "Walking into a studio with Max Martin or Gary Lightbody from Snow Patrol or Ed Sheeran—it was such an exciting rush."

Sheeran, for his part, probably felt exactly the same about working with Taylor, who was already an arena act when he released his first album, +, in 2011. After meeting in the summer of 2012 and co-writing the folk-pop ballad "Everything Has Changed" for *Red*, they developed a friendship that continues to this day. In a 2023 Apple Music interview, he said: "I had an hour-twenty conversation with her yesterday. Everything that was on our minds we talked about. It's kind of therapy [because] you're talking to someone who genuinely gets it."

She also wanted to involve Butch Walker, a singer-songwriter she met when he covered "You Belong With Me" from *Fearless*. It was just a bit of YouTube fun for him, but she heard it and was so taken with not just his cover but his "organic but emotionally charged" original songs that she invited him to perform with her at the 2010 Grammys. He coyly said he'd consider it as long as he was allowed to play his banjolin—a banjo/mandolin hybrid. She assented, and Walker, who had never before been to a Grammy ceremony, found himself backing her for a medley of "Today Was a Fairytale," "Rhiannon," and "You Belong With Me," the latter two featuring Stevie Nicks. Later, Swift gave Walker a gig on *Red*—he produced "Everything Has Changed."

When she re-recorded *Red* in 2021, Walker was one of the original producers she invited back—a feather in his cap, because not every producer returned. Working during one of the COVID-19 lockdowns, everyone—Swift, Sheeran, backing vocalist Gary Lightbody, and Walker, who had played most of the instruments on the 2012 recording—contributed their part remotely. He didn't see or even speak to Swift during the process.

Back in January 2012, as she and Borchetta discussed the songs that would become *Red*, Borchetta changed his mind about the album being "done." Listening to the title track, he thought the lyric and melody were great, but what it needed, he told Swift, was "a pop sound." Taylor and Chapman recorded it again and Borchetta was even less happy with that take. "And Taylor basically said, 'All right, would you call Max?'" he told *Time* in 2014.

He called Max. Her career had already gotten her a place in the record books, but that phone call would make everything that much sparklier. It would yield her first *Billboard* Hot 100 No. 1—"We Are Never Ever Getting Back Together," which would sell a record 623,000 downloads in its first week, the most ever sold in one week by a female artist—and a No. 2 single, "I Knew You Were Trouble," that shifted 7 million units. It added new elements to her sound, taking her to the borderline of pure pop—a border she would finally cross for good on her fifth album, *1989*.

Yet *Red* was still country enough to fetch 2014 Grammy nominations for Best Country Album and Best Country Song (for "Begin Again"). She also received a nomination in the Best Country Duo/Group Vocal Performance for "Highway Don't Care," a single she made with Tim McGraw and Keith Urban for McGraw's 2013 album *Two Lanes of Freedom*. McGraw had signed to Big Machine Records in 2012, so who better to guest on his first album for the label than Big Machine's resident superstar? The year before, there had been a Grammy nomination for Country Duo/Group for "Safe & Sound," a song she'd recorded with the country-folk duo The Civil Wars. It was surprise-released at the end of 2011, and while it didn't win the Duo/Group award, it did fetch the statuette for Best Song Written for Visual Media at the same ceremony. (It had been commissioned for the soundtrack of the first *Hunger Games* film.)

Going by Grammy nominations alone, there was still plenty of country in Swift's blood during the 2012–14 period. And yet . . . despite *Red*'s nod to her Nashville sound and the freelance projects with McGraw and The Civil Wars, the album truly was a last hurrah for the genre in which she started out. Notably, it was also nominated for the genre-neutral Album of the Year award in 2014 but lost to Daft Punk's *Random Access Memories*.

But first: What about "Red" itself, the song that impelled Borchetta to phone Martin? "Red" didn't get a pop treatment after all. It stayed in its country lane, and the final version features not just Swift and Chapman on production but another Nashville producer, Dann Huff, who had co-produced "Starlight" and "Begin Again." Nonetheless, Swift saw "Red" as a turning point; it was the song that, as she wrote it, made her wonder what she could come up with if she worked with people other than Chapman.

It also gave its name to the album, of course. The songs were mainly about "the tumultuous, crazy, insane, intense, semi-toxic relationships that I've experienced in the last two years," she said during a Google+ Hangout webchat on August 13, 2012. The emotions provoked by those romances veered between jealousy, adoration, and everything in between, and she saw all of them as red. It was the color of fire and of fiery feelings and summed up a period when her life had consisted of blazing ups and downs. As emphasis, the album sleeve showed her face in shadow except for her red-lipsticked mouth. That bright red became her everyday go-to; she still wears it now on the Eras Tour.

Swift and Borchetta couldn't have foreseen the influence Max Martin and his writing/production partner Shellback would have on her sound, not merely on *Red* but in the future. He and Shellback had created an enormously influential brand of electropop that dominated chart-pop in the 2000s and 2010s, and Swift was about to see what it could do for her. She met Martin (real name: Karl Sandberg) and Shellback (real name: Karl Johan Schuster; Martin calls him Johan) at Conway Recording in Los Angeles. As they discussed the session they were about to start, fate intervened in the shape of Maroon 5.

The group, who'd worked with Martin and Shellback on their 2012 album *Overexposed*, were recording in the next studio and a friend of theirs insisted on saying hello to Taylor. He was there to pass on a message from an ex-boyfriend, who apparently wanted Swift to call him. The friend cheerily said he'd heard that Swift and the ex were even considering making another go of things.

After he left, Swift explained to Martin that she'd had a tempestuous relationship with that particular ex, but she was sure of one thing. "We are never, *ever* getting back together," she told Martin, who related the anecdote during a 2018 Polar Music Awards video interview. Martin said: "And I was, like, 'That's pretty harsh.' [She replied:] 'No, we're never, ever, *ever* getting back together.' And I told her, 'That sounds like a song title.'" Then they began working on another tune, but when they resumed the next day, Swift had come up with ideas. She picked up her guitar and played them a melody, and Martin and Shellback pitched in. Twenty-five minutes later, they had a song. "We Are Never Ever Getting Back Together."

Naturally, when it appeared in August 2012 as *Red*'s lead single, there was a wave of speculation about the person she swore would never inveigle his way back into her heart. She's never named him, but she obviously enjoyed driving the message home via the track's scathing lyric and by telling interviewers what an impossible indie-rock snob he was. He'd made her insecure about her own music and musical taste. "He was the kind of dude who was, like, 'Oh, I just went and saw this basement concert, and there were only four people there, but they're starting to blow up now, so I'm really over it,'" she told

Australian radio station Nova FM. She was so affected by the implicit contempt for her own music that she actually wondered whether she should be playing smaller venues. But she didn't *want* to, she said—she was extremely happy to have a large following of people who loved her work and were endlessly supportive.

Although that relationship ended in what Swift described to *Vogue* in January 2012 as "absolute crash-and-burn heartbreak," she had more or less put the whole thing behind her by the time she wrote "Never Ever." And despite saying that the heartbreak would "turn out to be what the next album [*Red*] is about"—and that was essentially true—in the nine months between the *Vogue* story and *Red*'s release on October 22, she'd moved on. The problematic romance was history, and she was over it. At least, she was over it enough to be able to show her contempt for the guy on "Never Ever." And there was more. Encoded in the lyric was a succinct kiss-off: WHEN I STOPPED CARING WHAT YOU THOUGHT. Take that, buddy.

Predictably, *Red*'s most talked about tracks were the Martin/ Shellback collaborations: "Never Ever," "22," and "I Knew You Were Trouble." All were released as singles, and became the *Red* era's signature songs.

The other *Red* singles were the title track, "Begin Again," "Everything Has Changed," and "The Last Time." The last was a duet with Snow Patrol leader Gary Lightbody; they met in Los Angeles when Sheeran told Taylor that his mate Gary was in town—would it be all right if he dropped by the studio? That was typical of the serendipitous way Swift found musicians who would become significant collaborators. The way she and

Sheeran met, leading to a long and unbreakable friendship, was another example. While on the Australian leg of the Speak Now Tour in March 2012, she heard his single "Lego House" and liked it enough to write a line from the lyric on her left arm before her Sydney show. Sheeran heard about it, contacted her manager, and arranged to meet her later in the year. They hit it off so well that they wrote a song together, and now here they were.

When Sheeran invited Lightbody to meet Swift, who was then "obsessed" with Snow Patrol's music, she was bowled over when the Northern Irish singer broached the idea of their writing together for *Red*. Swift described "The Last Time"—a slow-simmering ballad not a million miles from a Snow Patrol track—as "intense."

At her request, it was produced and co-written by Dublin-born Jacknife Lee, chosen because Swift admired the dramatic sound he'd achieved with U2 and Lightbody's band. Lee recalled the session during a *Hot Press* interview in 2018. Swift went to his home studio in Topanga Canyon, near Los Angeles, and while she arrived with "bodyguards [and a] big black car," she was down to earth and got on with the task. As per her usual style, they wrote the song quickly and with little fuss, and she sang it on the sofa. "Then we had pasta for dinner and hung around with my kids," he said. "She was seeing Harry Styles at the time, so he came to Topanga on her recommendation."

She and Styles wrote "a few songs" together, but Lee didn't disclose what they were and it's hard to ascertain whether they've ever been used. They're not on Styles's three post–One Direction albums. At any event, Haylor—as they were inevitably dubbed on social media—were together for only a few months. They met in March 2012 at the Nickelodeon Kids' Choice Awards and began dating that November, splitting up in January 2013.

Though the Martin/Shellback songs grabbed the headlines, there was much more to *Red* than that. However, their contribution deserved the attention it got. "Never Ever" was her first unabashedly electropop song and became her first mainstream No. 1 single, while "I Knew You Were Trouble" was her second pop chart-topper—albeit on the Mainstream Top 40 chart rather than the Hot 100. It was singled out for special attention by listeners because of its dubstep bass drop, which Martin and Shellback had added when Swift sang them the bassline she wanted on the track. She confessed to knowing little about dubstep at that point—before "Trouble," the only time she'd heard it was when Sheeran, who was a fan, played her tracks he'd come across in UK clubs. But the Martin/Shellback dubstep intervention was so bold that Nora Princiotti of the *Every Single Album: Taylor Swift* podcast contended that it "change[d] the course of Taylor Swift's history . . . a dubstep beat from this woman who has been grounded in country music up to this point."

Indeed. But the rest of *Red* was sonically adventurous in its own way. Before we get to that, it's important to say that Swift didn't want to abandon the country industry—the press, radio stations, and fans who had been loyal since 2006— and she herself wasn't ready to make the leap into pure pop. Accordingly, *Red* has enough country and country-pop tracks to stave off accusations that she'd ditched them. Big Machine even sent a banjos-and-twang version of "Never Ever" to country radio. The *Speak Now* singles "Sparks Fly" and "Ours" had topped the Hot Country Songs chart, while the album had also been a country No. 1, so she was still among the genre's biggest names, and with the new tracks "Red," "Treacherous," and "Stay Stay Stay" she leaned into the kind of country-pop that could have appeared on *Speak Now*.

Elsewhere, though, the album bristles with change, as she tries on different styles. There was, as previously mentioned, the soft-rock stateliness of "The Last Time." There was the new-wave thrust of "Holy Ground," co-created with producer Jeff Bhasker, whose other major projects around that time were songs on albums by Lana Del Rey, Alicia Keys, and the Jay-Z/Kanye West collaboration *Watch the Throne*. There was bratty bubblegum in the shape of "22" (her age when she wrote it; it was panning out to be the best year of her life, she said). And the emotional soul of the record, "All Too Well," is a gently swelling acoustic-track-turned-power-ballad.

Red finishes by returning to country music. The sixteenth and final track, "Begin Again," is a soft meditation on the curative power of getting back on one's feet after a particularly hard breakup and finding new love. When Swift finds love, it's often—always?—the head-over-heels kind, as she told *Marie Claire*: "You make eye contact with someone across the room and it clicks and, bam, you're there." That's exactly what happens in the hazy, filmic "Begin Again" video: Taylor is in Paris, newly single and missing the man she thought loved her. We see her sitting on the bank of the Seine, then pensively sipping *un café* in a bar. A handsome photographer spots her across the room and joins her; by the last scene, the impossibly beautiful twosome are wandering through cobbled back streets and Swift is shyly smiling, unable to believe that, just as she was mourning the end of one relationship, a new one is starting. Even if she sometimes loves not wisely but too well, she's lucky: she can always write a song about it.

She intended "Begin Again" to act as a bookend, with *Red*'s opening track "State of Grace" providing the other. She chose them not because they were musically similar—they're not. "State of Grace" verges on arena-rock, while "Begin Again" is a pretty country ballad. The commonality is in their subject matter, both being about a particular relationship she felt had "damaged" her. But "Begin Again" closes the album on a hopeful note and was written at a time when she really had met someone new.

As ever, Swift didn't shed any light on who she was dating, but the album provided hints. The coded message in the lyric to "Everything Has Changed" was HYANNIS PORT, and in "Starlight," the next track, it was FOR ETHEL. Only Americans of a certain age would have known what they meant; for those too young to have heard of Ethel Kennedy, widow of the assassinated Senator Robert Kennedy, they offered a history lesson. The Kennedy Compound at Hyannis Port, Massachusetts, is Mrs. Kennedy's home to this day and was visited by Swift in the summer of 2012 after she struck up a friendship with Ethel's daughter Rory. Swift had admired Ethel long before she knew Rory and had written "Starlight" about Robert and Ethel's 1940s courtship. Swift asked to meet Ethel, and the two hit it off. Mrs. Kennedy invited her to the Kennedys' Fourth of July party at Hyannis Port, where she met seventeen-year-old Conor, grandson of the senator.

(In the interests of completeness, we note here that more than a few Swifties believe the new love affair alluded to in "Begin Again" involved not Conor Kennedy but Will Anderson of Virginia pop-rockers Parachute. The evidence in favor was that in the summer of 2012, he and Swift had had a coffee date and their movements that day—laughing in a café, walking to her car—seemed to match the lyric of "Begin Again." Anderson shrugged off talk of a relationship. He and Swift were friends, nothing more, he said on the Ralphie Aversa radio show. But had he actually asked Swift whether "Begin Again" was about him? "We don't really talk about that stuff . . . we talk about professional stuff.")

Though the relationship with Conor lasted only a few months, Swift was so taken with Hyannis Port's windswept beauty that she bought a house nearby in November 2012. *The Cape Cod Times* reported that a company called Ocean Drive LLC paid $4.8 million for the seven-bedroom beachfront property, and the buyer appeared to be acting for Swift. Ethel Kennedy believed so—she told the *Times*: "I am happy that we'll all be neighbors." While Swift did renovate parts of the house, she never moved in, however, and in February 2013, as reported by *E! News*, the house was sold for $5.6 million.

But she was smitten with the New England coastline, and in April 2013 she bought a house in the Watch Hill area of Westerly, Rhode Island. Car-maker Henry Ford and actor Clark Gable were previous Watch Hill residents; the eight-bedroom mansion for which Swift reportedly paid $17 million had once belonged to an heiress to the Standard Oil fortune, Rebekah Harkness. A socialite and dance patron, Harkness owned the house, which she named Holiday House, between 1948 and 1974 and hosted lavish parties there. Having been told about her by the estate agent who showed her through the house, Swift was fascinated. She was especially drawn to what she saw as similarities between Harkness and herself. While Harkness occupied a very different level of social notoriety—endlessly upsetting the neighbors, she cleaned her swimming pool with champagne and had a group of friends she called the Bitch Pack—Swift admired her, she told *People* in 2021, for "own[ing] her desires and wildness."

Starting in July 2013, she continued the Harkness party tradition by holding Fourth of July gatherings at Holiday House (its official name is High Watch), for a group of friends who came to be known as her Squad. She also—what else?— wrote a song about Harkness, "The Last Great American Dynasty." It appeared on *Folklore*, the first of her two 2020 "pandemic albums."

The Holiday House sale went through a few weeks after the first date of Swift's Red Tour, which launched at Omaha's CenturyLink Center on March 13. When it wrapped in Singapore on June 12, 2014, it had grossed $150 million and been named the top-grossing country tour of all time. Equally importantly, reviews for the two-hour spectacular—it featured multiple stages, stairways, and catwalks, and no fewer than eleven costume changes—acknowledged that, as *Rolling Stone*'s Rob Sheffield put it: "No other pop auteur can touch her right now."

The tour also became known for an incident before the show at the Pepsi Center in Denver on June 2, 2013. It saw

Swift react quickly and decisively when she was inappropriately touched at a meet-and-greet before the show. Posing for a picture with employees of local country-radio station KYGO, she felt David Mueller, a presenter who had joined the station five months before, raise her skirt and grab her backside. Swift immediately reported it to Andrea Swift, who was traveling with her, and her security guard. Mueller denied it but was sacked by the station two days later. The incident might have ended there if Mueller hadn't sued Swift for defamation in September 2015. Swift countersued for assault. When the case was tried in 2017, Swift repeated her claim. "He grabbed my ass underneath my skirt. He stayed attached to my bare ass cheek as I lurched away from him," she said, and told Mueller's lawyer: "I'm not going to allow you or your client to make me feel in any way that this is my fault." The jury found in favor of Swift, awarding her $1—the symbolic recompense she had requested. That single dollar sent a vehement message to women in the #MeToo era: Swift was uninterested in financial gain; she was motivated by knowing that her fans would see her refusing to let an assault go unchallenged.

The Red Tour was also the birthplace of a feud that would rumble on until 2019 and inspire a song—"Bad Blood"—that became a No. 1 single. Though Swift has never named the other party, it is widely thought to have been Katy Perry. In brief, the beef involved dancers Swift hired for the tour, who gave notice to Swift before the end of the tour that they were leaving to join Perry's own tour.

Swift was guarded about the details, but she did tell *Rolling Stone* in September 2014 that "Bad Blood" was about a female artist who "tried to hire a bunch of people out from under me." A year later, though, she gave *GQ* a different story. It was really about an ex-boyfriend, she claimed, not a female singer. She hadn't wanted to drop the guy in it—they were now on good terms, and she felt protective. So she'd come up with a diversionary tactic, saying that the song's subject was a friend. And that was the (convoluted) story behind "Bad Blood," she said.

If the spat really involved Perry—and Perry said it did, during an appearance on the Carpool Karaoke segment of *The Late Late Show with James Corden* in 2017—it started on the Red Tour in 2013. Swift offered jobs to three dancers who had worked on Perry's 2011–12 California Dreams tour, during which they became close friends with Perry. They told Perry about Swift's offer and asked if she minded. Because Perry wasn't then promoting an album, she encouraged the dancers to take the work, which would start in March 2013. There was one proviso: Perry was due to start her next promotional cycle in about a year and asked the dancers to ensure there was a clause in their contracts that would allow them to leave Swift's tour when necessary, with thirty days' notice.

Perry's Prismatic world tour, which was linked to her October 2013 album *Prism*, began on May 7, 2014. The Red Tour, meanwhile, was scheduled to end on June 12. Because Red took a hiatus in May, the dancers weren't needed until May 30 in Shanghai. But that same day, Perry would be playing the O2 Arena in London. In all, only seven Red dates conflicted with Prismatic, but Perry needed the dancers to begin rehearsals months earlier. One dancer, Lockhart Brownlie, told the

Examiner that he and the others had been with Taylor for the first six months of Red, then left to rehearse with Perry.

Feeling let down by a woman she'd considered a friend, Swift was deeply upset. She dealt with it as she'd always dealt with slings and arrows: by writing about it. "Bad Blood" took shape in 2013, as she toured *Red*, and would become *1989*'s third No. 1 single in 2015. (The song is discussed in Chapter 10.)

Her support act on Red's North American leg, Ed Sheeran, also reaped substantial benefits from being on the tour. He played to upward of 15,000 people a night, and there could hardly have been a better advertisement for his own talent and for the + album. It was the last time a Swift tour would be classified "country"—the next time she took a show on the road, which would be in May 2015, the set list was dominated by pop tracks from the next album, *1989*, and very few early songs made the cut.

By 2015, she was such a pop powerhouse that she was able to secure the services of Mick Jagger for a surprise high-energy duet of "Satisfaction" at the September 26 Nashville date. Jagger was returning a favor: three months earlier, Swift had joined the Rolling Stones onstage in Chicago for a touchingly pretty rendition of "As Tears Goes By." In a video interview backstage after the duet, Swift mused: "The way that you see them [the Stones] give everything they have for every single performance, that's what makes fans loyal to them and that's been a huge influence on my outlook on my entire career."

Before all that, however, was the release of *Red* on October 22. Wary of pre-release leaks, Taylor and Borchetta swore every one of the album's personnel to secrecy about the songs—rehearsing for a string of TV performances set to take place shortly after the album appeared, Swift and her band only rehearsed the tracks that were already out as singles. They didn't play any of the other twelve for fear of somehow being overheard and the new songs leaking.

It didn't happen. *Red* made its appearance as scheduled and promptly racked up the highest first-week sales of any album since Eminem's *Encore*, which racked up 1.5 million in its opening week in 2004. As with *Speak Now*, it was sold in left-field places. Along with the usual record shops, fans (or curious non-fans) could pick it up at Starbucks, Papa Johns Pizza, and Walgreens.

It's customary for reviewers to receive a new album in advance so they're able to live with it for a while before writing their review. Not this album. They got it at the same time as the public and had to compose articles more or less immediately. Some immediately understood what Swift was trying to do, and that was reflected in their reviews: "Not just catchy but compelling," said AllMusic; *The AV Club*'s opinion was "magnificent at times but also complicated." But there was so much to take in—such a mix of styles—that some publications found it hard to get a handle on the album. "Disjointed," was PopMatters' verdict, while the *Telegraph* wavered, pronouncing some tracks excellent but feeling that the LP as a whole was "disjointed" and "bloated."

Was she bothered? Unlikely.

CHAPTER 10

1989

The 1989 World Tour, which ran from May 5 to December 12, 2015—the day before Swift's twenty-sixth birthday—was, on the surface, just another jaunt around the arenas and stadiums of three continents. It took in $250 million and was 2015's highest grossing tour. So far, so Swift. Yet it was also the tour that declared her position at the absolute center of 2010s popular culture. The guests who shared the stage during the nightly "surprise" slot reflected that: Julia Roberts, Joan Baez, Chris Rock, Serena Williams, and Kobe Bryant were just five of the figureheads who joined Swift to sing with her or just dance along.

Baez, one of America's great folk singers, and Roberts, winner of three Golden Globes and an Academy Award, found themselves dancing together to the *1989* single "Style" before 50,000 fans at Levi's Stadium in Santa Clara, California, on August 15. It was a pairing no one could have foreseen, but such was Swift's reach and persuasiveness that it happened. Roberts, for one, had been unprepared for the intensity of being onstage at a pop concert—but then, it wasn't just any pop concert. She later told *Extra* that it had been "one of those crazy, out-of-body moments."

"Crazy, out-of-body moments" could just as well have applied to the entire *1989* era. It saw Swift complete her transition to pop, resoundingly defy the 2010s trend of declining record sales, and flex her activist muscles when streaming services allowed listeners free access to music on ad-supported free tiers, thus shrinking "the number of paid album sales drastically," as she wrote in the *Wall Street Journal* in July 2014. The icing on the cake was being named, with new boyfriend Calvin Harris, the "highest-paid celebrity couple" of 2015. *Forbes* estimated their combined earnings at $146 million, beating 2014's best-paid couple, Beyoncé and Jay-Z. On his own, producer/songwriter/DJ Harris also topped a *Forbes* list of the world's top-earning DJs, titled "Electronic Cash Kings"— and cash is what he brought in: the former Marks & Spencer fruit buyer from Dumfries commanded up to $1 million to play a private party, and $400,000 per night at his Las Vegas residencies. That was eclipsed by Joel "deadmau5" Zimmerman's reported $425,000 nightly fee, but Zimmerman was lumbered with having to wear a huge, mouse-eared helmet during his sets.

While Swift's earnings were the most obvious marker of her success—and it was a level of success that gave her access to the highest echelons of the music industry and beyond—it was what she did with her stature that counted. Some pop stars buy real estate and cars, which she did, but they don't use their clout in less material ways. She did. On November 4, 2014, she used hers to draw the industry's attention to an issue that had become not so much the elephant in the room as the saber-toothed tiger voraciously digesting artists' earnings.

That was the week *1989* entered the chart at No. 1— released on October 27, it sold 1.28 million copies in its first seven days. On November 4, Swift removed her music from Spotify. Her *Wall Street Journal* leader piece three months earlier had in a sense led to this; it set out her views about streaming services and piracy and how they had changed the public's perception of music's value. If the question was, "Should music be free?" her answer was a vehement, "Absolutely not." She was up against a behemoth: file-sharing and, later, legal streaming platforms such as Spotify offered all the music anyone could want without charge. (Spotify has an ad-free premium tier, which users pay for, but its no-cost option, supported by ads, is immensely popular.)

Album sales were already suffering from digital downloading, which made it possible for users to buy one or two tracks from an album rather than the whole record. Streaming enabled them to hear whatever they liked without spending any money at all. Swift wrote that she had observed with dismay some major artists try to stem the bleeding by giving away their music as part of promotions or tie-ups with brands. Two months after her article appeared, U2 did pretty much that, giving away their 2014 album, *Songs of Innocence*, as a gift to iTunes' 500 million users. It was added to their libraries as a surprise— and Apple then had to provide a tool for deleting it when many users protested its arrival. However, the musicians Swift wrote about weren't "gifting" albums; they were cutting promotional deals and tie-ups to get their albums into people's homes and iPods at a difficult time for recorded music. "Music is art, and art is important and rare," she wrote. "Important, rare things are valuable. Valuable things should be paid for. It's my opinion that music should not be free." Swift returned her catalogue to Spotify in 2017, as a thank-you to fans when *1989* sold its 10 millionth copy.

But even as Swift wrote about other artists offering promotional deals, she herself was having to provide extras to give her records and tours added value. She revealed that the reason the Red Tour had been packed with surprise guests was that nearly everyone in the audience would have already seen the show online, so Swift wanted to give them something special.

In June 2015, she spoke out again. The new streaming service Apple Music was offering users a three-month free trial, during which artists would not be paid royalties. In an open letter to Apple, she pointed out the unfairness; she was ready to withhold *1989* from the platform if the tech giant didn't pay artists. The next day, Apple Music reversed its no-royalties policy.

When Swift set about making *1989*, she had a clear vision for her fifth album. Or rather, she had several ideas that she intended would cohere into an album. They involved a complete change of scene, to which end she moved to New York in April 2014—a huge resettlement after a decade in Nashville but one that she'd been edging toward for several years. "I dreamt about moving to New York. I obsessed about moving to New York, and then I did it," she told *Good Morning America* in October 2014. And she did it in style. Her Tribeca duplex lofts—plural; she bought two adjacent properties for a reported $19.9 million—were vast and airy and furnished to be simultaneously homey and awe-inspiring. Their former owner, *Lord of the Rings* director Peter Jackson, bought them in 2008 for $17.3 million but didn't combine them; almost as soon as Swift entered into a contract with Jackson, in February 2014, she planned renovations that would turn them into a single ten-bed, ten-bath property. Part of it became an apartment for her security team.

Like millions of other new arrivals, she saw NYC as "a place of endless potential and possibilities," and she wrote the sleek synthpopper "Welcome to New York"—a rather romanticized view of living in the Big Apple but one brimming with excitement. It's the first track on *1989*; a review in PopMatters pronounced it "a manifesto," and the song, full of wonder and freedom, does set the scene for an album that Swift called "a kind of rebirth for me." It was also a signpost indicating the musical direction of the following twelve tracks. A clue in the song is the Juno-106 synthesizer used by co-producer Ryan Tedder. It's "a very 1980s keyboard," he told *Entertainment Weekly*, because Swift had given him a brief: she wanted an eighties feel. In fact, she wanted it to encompass the whole album.

Swift had been inspired by the sonically adventurous yet populist chart music that was ubiquitous in her birth year, 1989, and decided to construct a sound that wasn't a million miles distant. In an ABC News/Yahoo News live stream on August 18, 2014, she explained the thought process behind the record: "I've been listening to a lot of late-eighties pop because I loved how bold and ahead of its time it was." She saw it as rebellious and emblematic of a time when it was possible to create bright sonic palettes that weren't just catchy but futuristic and often socially progressive (think, for example, of The Communards, whose name was inspired by the revolutionary nineteenth-century Paris Commune, or the Soho hit "Hippychick," which referenced the mid-eighties miners' strike). Swift saw the period as a time of great potential: "The idea of endless possibility was kind of a theme of the last year of my life."

It amounted to looking back in order to go forward, which might have spawned an argument about whether it was unimaginative to base a 2014 record on a twenty-five-year-old sound. Might have, but didn't. Anyone old enough to remember the eighties would have nostalgically tapped a toe when they heard the likes of "Shake It Off" or "Blank Space"—their hyper-glossy, synth-based production felt comfortingly familiar, conjuring up an era. Few saw it as an excuse to criticize Swift, because she carried it off so well. That's what counted; as the *Guardian*'s Alexis Petridis wrote in a four-star review of the album: "Its sound is a lovingly done reboot of . . . late-eighties MTV pop-rock."

In any event, it didn't matter. The youngest Swifties, born in the 2000s, had no throwback memories: to them, *1989* was a fresh new vibe. And their moms, who liked what they heard of *1989*, started to become fans too. The *1989* era was when adults finally took notice of Swift's musicianship and began to accompany their daughters to shows not merely to keep an eye on them but to hear the music. Any parental qualms about Swift's fitness as a role model were undoubtedly quashed by her girl-next-door sweetness: "Every artist has their set of priorities. Being looked at as sexy? Not really on my radar. But nice? I really hope that that is the impression," she told the *Guardian* in an interview that coincided with the August 19 release of *1989*'s first single, "Shake It Off."

And she wasn't the only young star to release music that hinged on a back-to-the-future feel. Dua Lipa would do the same in 2020 with her disco-referencing second LP, *Future Nostalgia*—a career-changing hit for her. Generally considered to be among Swift's best albums, *1989* topped critics' poll after critics' poll. Its allure was neatly summarized by *Esquire*: it fused "Swiftian heartbreak [and] pop euphoria"—as simple and powerful as that.

Swift had been motivated by the "bright colors, bold chances [and] rebellion" of eighties pop, but her interest in the era had been awakened by something else. Every day that she worked on *1989*, she was consumed by the need "to make a new style of music than I'd ever made before," she said during the ABC/Yahoo live stream. Not one to do things by halves, Swift held the live stream, which had an in-person audience of around thirty fans and was watched by a much larger online audience, in the Empire State Building. Having obeyed her heart and moved to New York, she was now immersing herself in the life of the city, so where else to have the event but its most iconic building? To introduce it, she even ventured onto an open walkway on the 103rd floor, just under the building's spire. It looked, and apparently was, terrifying. "As cool as this is—and you can see all of New York, it's a beautiful day—to be honest with you, it's kind of scary up here," she said. Nonetheless, her passion for her new town got her appointed New York's official Welcome Ambassador for Tourism.

It was important to Swift that *1989* be "sonically cohesive" in a way that *Red* wasn't. Rather than using multiple producers as per *Red* and making a record that was criticized by some for having no core identity—neither quite country nor quite pop— she was going to fully commit to pop. The first song she wrote for the new album, in October 2012, was a hello and a goodbye: the big synth-ballad "This Love," composed on her own (it would be the only completely self-composed track on the record). Hello to her new sound; goodbye to Nathan Chapman, who produced it but amicably parted with her after that one song.

The producers she chose for the rest of the album were Max Martin and Shellback, Ryan Tedder, English singer-songwriter Imogen Heap, and Jack Antonoff. The latter, singer-guitarist of Bleachers and Fun, had previously written a song with Swift, "Sweeter Than Fiction," for the 2013 film *One Chance*. He worked on only two *1989* tracks ("I Wish You Would" and "Out of the Woods") but was henceforth one of Swift's favorite collaborators, sharing a sense of humor and seeing eye-to-eye on musical decisions.

The album ended up containing several songs that were both huge hits at the time and became canonical works. "Shake It Off," "Blank Space," and "Bad Blood," all No. 1 singles, are known by people who wouldn't know what a Swiftie was; they were simply ubiquitous radio songs. When *The New York Times* titled its review of *1989* "A Farewell to Twang," there was a sweet sadness to the words, as if the reviewer knew Swift would never return to the twang. But just as she had sensed back in 2004, that there was an untapped young audience who would listen to country music if one of their peers sang it, she now knew she wouldn't develop further as an artist if she didn't move to pop. "I've never made these kind of changes before," she told the ABC/Yahoo audience. "This is my very first official documented pop album." By bluntly announcing it, she got the attention of the media and fans but also roped in uncommitted bystanders who hadn't bought into her country incarnation.

One of her first actions as she geared up to promote *1989* was to cut her hair. Nashville-girl curls and winsome fringes: gone. In their place, a sharp urban "lob"—a collarbone-length long bob. It's visible in the "Shake It Off" video, though the video was more renowned for its multiple costumes and the storyline of Swift pitting her deliberately inept dance moves against those of professional breakdancers, ballerinas, and twerkers. The point: it's more important to dance with your whole heart, however clumsily, than to be the best. The track, a co-write with Max Martin and Shellback, was a vibrant, immensely catchy dance track that stared her critics in the face—those who minutely scrutinized her life and said she was dim and had too many boyfriends—and said, "I don't care." It debuted at No. 1 in the Hot 100—the first time one of her tracks had gone straight in at the top—and spent four weeks there.

The next single, "Blank Space" (out November 10), was spare, cool dance-pop that had Swift sending up the media-concocted image of her as a romantic "psychopath" (her word). It replaced "Shake It Off" at No. 1 in the Hot 100, making her the first woman to replace herself at the top of the US chart, and stayed at the top for seven weeks.

In the midst of all this came the release of *1989* itself. It wasn't just her first pop album, it was the first album she had made about being famous. She still wrote about the pain of being ditched by someone she loved, as on the third single "Style," which might have been about her romance with Harry Styles—but its video was simply an homage to being young and stunning and didn't conjure up anyone in particular. (Note: the clattering electrodance album track "Out of the Woods" was almost definitely about Styles, referencing a snowmobile accident on a December 2012 skiing holiday that left him needing twenty stitches in his chin.)

And "Bad Blood," of course, was about a top-flight pop star rivalry. Its video was where Swift really showed us how different life was for the famous: in it, her character, Catastrophe, battled an archenemy called Arsyn (played by Selena Gomez) and was supported by a group of famous women who were now central figures in her social circles. It was a highly enjoyable *Avengers*-style action video that showed a girl can rely on her friends to have her back—especially if the friends were Lena Dunham, Gigi Hadid, Cara Delevingne, and a dozen other big names. (It turned out later that actress-singer Zendaya, who played Cut Throat, was there because Swift—whom she didn't know well—thought she was cool.) The sole male in the video, playing Welvin da Great, was Kendrick Lamar, who rapped on the single remix.

The feud behind "Bad Blood," by the way, finally came to an end in 2018, when Perry sent Swift an olive branch—not a symbolic branch, but a real one. Swift responded on Instagram: "Thank you, Katy." Fans knew the spat had really ended when Perry appeared in the video for the 2019 single "You Need to

Calm Down"—she was dressed as a hamburger and Swift as a side of fries.

Straight in at No. 1, *1989* would have done so even without promotions like bonus tracks and extras that encouraged fans to buy the physical CD rather than downloading the album. Nonetheless, 616,000 people downloaded it in its first week. Fans who sprang for the compact disc received a set of five Polaroid photos of Swift, which reflected the fact that she had been an enthusiastic Polaroid user for the past few years. The album's cover shot was also a Polaroid—a misty, milky shot of her body from the waist up, with the top half of her face not shown. The record won the 2016 Grammy for Album of the Year—she was the first woman to win it twice—and Pop Vocal Album, and the striking "Bad Blood" video took home Best Music Video.

Though Swift began the *1989* era a single woman, she began dating Calvin Harris after being introduced by Ellie Goulding at the *Elle* Style Awards in February 2015. Goulding noted that both were "really awesome and . . . really tall." Swift characterized it as "a magic relationship," and they were together until June 2016. During that time, they co-wrote the April 2016 single "This Is What You Came For," sung by Rihanna and a No. 2 hit in the UK. To prevent the song being overshadowed by their fame as a couple, Swift used the pseudonym Nils Sjöberg—chosen, she said, because they were two of the most popular Swedish names.

She and Harris broke up reasonably amicably—"It clearly wasn't right, so it ended," he told *GQ*—but fell out a few weeks later when her involvement with the song came to light. Swift might never have revealed that she was Nils Sjöberg had Harris not implied during a radio interview that she hadn't been involved in creating the song. He was a guest on the *On Air with Ryan Seacrest* program on April 29, 2016, the day "This Is What You Came For" was released and was asked, "Will you do a collaboration with your girlfriend?" Harris replied: "You know, we haven't even spoken about it. I can't see it happening, though. She's about to take a long break, you know?" (At that point, Swift had finished the *1989* promotional cycle and won the Album of the Year Grammy, after which she lapsed into a rare fallow period, unsure how to follow up its success.)

Though she and Harris had agreed to keep Sjöberg's identity secret, she reportedly felt that Harris had gone too far, and this seemingly precipitated their breakup two months later. Then, in July, a Swift representative confirmed to *People* that she had co-written the song. Harris took that as a dig and retaliated with a series of tweets he later deleted. Though he praised her in one, posted on July 13—"Amazing lyric writer and she smashed it as usual"—he was less upbeat in others: "I figure if you're happy in your new relationship you should focus on that instead of trying to tear your ex bf down." (Swift had begun dating English actor Tom Hiddleston shortly after splitting with Harris.) Two months later, the tweets deleted and his equilibrium restored, Harris looked back on the uncharacteristic outburst as a moment of "succumb[ing] to pressure," he told *British GQ*. The pair eventually mended fences and communicated occasionally via text.

Did Swift write about their relationship on her next album, *Reputation*? Hard to say. When it came out in November

2017, it was difficult to pinpoint any songs that addressed it. There was media speculation about the electro-grunge track "I Did Something Bad," though it's hard to imagine its scathing references to playboys and narcissists describing the mild-mannered Harris; "Getaway Car," a sugar-sweet synthpopper, was also named because it mentioned a black-tie event, which some thought was about the May 2016 Met Ball, a splashy fashion event in New York where Swift met Hiddleston. A "getaway car" was what Swift supposedly wanted so she could leave her relationship with Harris.

She and Hiddleston quickly acquired the awkward portmanteau Hiddleswift, and spent the summer of 2016 together. The highest profile moment of their relationship took place at Swift's Rhode Island house during the Fourth of July weekend. They splashed in the surf, the main attraction of a group that included models Gigi Hadid and Karlie Kloss, actresses Blake Lively and Ruby Rose, and the pop trio Haim. Hiddleston happened to be wearing a white tank top printed with the words "I Heart TS" and also had a temporary bicep tattoo of the letter T inside a heart (Swift had a matching one). He quickly felt the full force of social-media ridicule. Some considered his display of adoration—"I Heart TS"—too demonstrative to be real and assumed the relationship was a "showmance" (it wasn't); others found it funny. The *Daily Telegraph*'s arts and entertainment editor Anita Singh tweeted: "Tomorrow: Tom Hiddleston appears in Taylor Swift video, dressed as Taylor Swift. Next week: Tom Hiddleston changes name to 'Taylor Swift.'"

Asked by the *Hollywood Reporter* whether the relationship was a publicity stunt, Hiddleston couldn't have sounded more mild-mannered English male. "Well, um. How best to put this? That notion is—look, the truth is that Taylor Swift and I are together, and we're very happy. Thanks for asking. That's the truth. It's not a publicity stunt."

In March 2017, Hiddleston told *GQ* why he'd worn the TS tank top: "We were playing a game and I slipped and hurt my back. I wanted to protect the graze from the sun and said, 'Does anyone have a T-shirt?' And one of her friends said, 'I've got this.'" Everyone at the party thought it was hilarious and took it as the joke it was. But the top became a symbol of their relationship, and he was embarrassed by the jibes. Having only begun dating in May, the pair were still in the getting-to-know-you stage; they'd met each other's parents but were a long way from settling down. In the event, the relationship ended in September—amicably, both said.

In that first half of 2016, she was also involved with two non-*1989* projects. She co-wrote "I Don't Wanna Live Forever" for the soundtrack of the 2017 film *Fifty Shades Darker* and sang it with Zayn Malik, formerly of One Direction. It was to be the last song she released, in December 2016, before the *Reputation* era got underway. Meanwhile, a song she wrote for *Red*, "Better Man," was repurposed when she sent it to the harmony-based country group Little Big Town. Their plaintive version, released in October 2016, won a 2018 Grammy for Best Country Duo/Group Performance, but those wanting to hear Swift sing it had to wait until she re-recorded *Red* in 2021 and released "Better Man" as a From the Vault bonus track.

In April 2016 came the uproar set off by Kanye West when he said Swift had given permission for him to call her a "bitch" on his new single, "Famous." It was a knotty, unedifying feud (described in more detail in Chapter 1) that ended in vindication for Swift when a recording of her phone call with West was released in 2020 and showed she had not given permission. Before that, though, the fallout led to Swift being vilified in some quarters when it appeared that she was lying.

She was already coping with her mother having been diagnosed with breast cancer in April 2015 and now was enduring "a mass public shaming, with millions of people saying you are quote-unquote canceled." She was speaking to *Vogue* in the summer of 2019, two albums down the line (*1989* was followed by *Reputation* in 2017 and *Lover* in 2019), but it was clear the memories still stung. "[It was a] very isolating experience . . . I don't think there are that many people who can actually understand what it's like to have millions of people hate you very loudly."

In the 2020 documentary *Miss Americana*, she would look back at her 2016–17 pariah period, which generated sneering Twitter hashtags like #TaylorSwiftIsOverParty: "Nobody physically saw me for a year. That's what I thought they wanted. It woke me up from constantly feeling I was fighting for people's respect." That wasn't entirely true. She didn't spend that year a complete recluse. She still had a social life, and if she wasn't as visible as usual, it was partly due to the *1989* promotional cycle having ended; she released no solo music between *1989*'s final single, "New Romantics," in February 2016 and *Reputation*'s first salvo, "Look What You Made Me Do," in August 2017.

In the autumn of 2016, after the fling with Hiddleston, she began a new relationship with another English actor, Joe Alwyn.

She's said to have met him on May 2 that year at the Met Gala, the annual New York event known as "the Oscars of fashion." Swift co-hosted with Idris Elba, who later said there was mild embarrassment when he and Swift walked through the crowd: Kanye West and Kim Kardashian were there. "And I was, like, 'Oh, this is awks,'" he told the *The New York Times* in 2017. He hadn't known there was bad blood between them but sensed a mood. Otherwise, he said, he'd had a great time.

For the next six years, Taylor would spend much of her downtime with Alwyn in London. Determined to keep the paparazzi off their trail, she rarely went out in public with him and also reduced the number of events she attended alone. Where she did appear, it was mainly work-related. Early in the relationship, in October 2016, she showed her face at Drake's thirtieth birthday party but thereafter confined most appearances to performances. Those included her only singing date of 2016, at the Formula 1 Grand Prix in Austin, Texas, and a pre–Super Bowl concert in Houston in February 2017. She also became less active on social media—previously her primary channel for connecting with fans—and stopped posting photos of herself. It was even suggested that she was using chartered planes, rather than her own jet, to defeat plane-tracker apps.

Despite feeling isolated, and still reeling from being at the sharp end of an unjustified pile-on, she put her frazzled emotional state and isolation to good use, creating *Reputation*.

CHAPTER 11

Reputation

Swift had always left a two-year gap between albums. She'd always done plenty of press in the lead-up to an album and filled her social media with chatty communiques to fans and friends. That was the old Taylor. The August 2017 lead-up to *Reputation* drew a line between that Taylor and a new, near-unrecognizable version. The Old Taylor—so-named in the album's first single, "Look What You Made Me Do"— was the best friend you'd never met, the girl in the Tribeca-penthouse-next-door, the reliably sweet young woman who also happened to be globally famous. The new Taylor wasn't taking it anymore.

On August 18, she did the unthinkable. Her social media accounts? Blanked out. When her then 102 million Instagram followers (there are now 283 million) checked in, they found a blank page and the words: "No posts yet." Her website showed only a black screen. That was a Friday. After leaving fans to stew all weekend, on Monday she posted a fifteen-second video clip of a writhing snake's tail. On Tuesday its body was shown. On Wednesday, its head appeared, tongue flickering and red eyes balefully glowering. Her intentions became apparent later that day, in a new Instagram post: "Reputation. The new album from Taylor Swift. November 10." "Reputation" was written in a gothic font against a black background, and the theme was carried over into her new single, which came out the next day, August 24.

Its video, onscreen from August 27 when it premiered at the MTV Video Music Awards, opens in a graveyard at midnight. The camera zooms toward an ivy-covered gravestone: "Here lies Taylor Swift's reputation." Swift, made up as an authentically alarming zombie, climbs out of the grave and digs another— for herself, or the self she was in the *1989* era. Already heaving with symbolism, the video goes on to reveal snake jewelry, a Grammy, and an MTV award, a golden cage in which she's trapped. One scene is set at "Squad U" (Squad University, a hitherto unknown institution where—presumably—beautiful actresses and models graduate to being members of Taylor's circle) and another scene is in a ballroom, in which eight male dancers wear tight cropped tops sequined with "I Heart TS."

Both the snake jewels and Squad U sardonically referenced aspects of her life that had agitated detractors in the past eighteen months. The existence of the Squad—or at least its members' casual use of that word to identify themselves— was especially inflammatory to some, as was the #SquadGoals hashtag they sometimes used. She was taken to task for it as early as 2015, a year before her life was upended by the wrangle with Kanye West over "Famous." Referring to the

West situation in an interview with *Time* after the magazine named her its Person of the Year 2023, she said: "You have a fully manufactured frame job, in an illegally recorded phone call, which Kim Kardashian edited and then put out to say to everyone that I was a liar."

The snake video clips that preceded the *Reputation* announcement were thought to be a poke at Kardashian, who had tweeted on July 17, 2016: "Wait it's legit National Snake Day?!?!? They have holidays for everybody, I mean everything these days!" It was followed by thirty-seven snake emojis and received nearly 350,000 likes. (World—not National—Snake Day really exists. It's an annual "opportunity to celebrate snakes and raise awareness about their preservation." Observed on July 16 (not 17), it asks the public to "help end the stigma around snakes.")

The same day, Kardashian released edited, secretly recorded clips on Snapchat of her husband's phone conversation with Swift—the conversation at the heart of the feud between Taylor and the couple. The purpose of Kardashian releasing the clips in July was to prove that Swift and her husband really had talked on the phone—though the footage didn't contain any discussion of "bitch." Despite that, as soon as it went live on Snapchat, thousands took it as "proof" that Swift had been lying. For the next year, Swift's social media posts were met with thousands of snake emojis from supporters of Kardashian and West, who thought she had betrayed the rapper. As detailed in Chapter 1, Swift was vindicated in 2020, when a full recording of the phone call found its way online and verified her version of events.

Before that happened, all Swift could do was make the best of things. On the Reputation Stadium Tour, which ran from May 8 to November 21, 2018, she seized the chance to show the world exactly how bothered she was. In an article she wrote for *Elle* in March 2019, Swift said: "I had to keep from laughing every time my 63-foot inflatable cobra named Karyn appeared onstage in front of 60,000 screaming fans." A lesson, there, in dealing with "haters": reclaim the snake while reminding them that you sell 60,000 tickets a night. By the end of the tour, she could also enjoy the fact that the US/Canada leg had broken the record held by the Rolling Stones since 2007 for the top-grossing North American tour in history. She would break her own record in 2023–24 with the billion-dollar Eras Tour, the highest-grossing ever.

Returning to 2016: Kardashian's Snapchat posts were the immediate cause of her "takedown," but public disquiet about the Squad had preceded it. In an August 2015 *Guardian* opinion piece, writer Judnick Maynard accused the Squad of cultural appropriation for thoughtlessly lifting both "squad" and "#SquadGoals" from Black culture. The terms had been used since at least the late noughties: a "squad" was a friendship group and "squad goals" an empowering marshaling call to the group. The subhead of the article accused "the privileged and assuming behavior of overdogs like Taylor Swift" of being responsible for the "whitewashing" of Black cultural trends.

A word on the Squad: in the 2010s, Swift made female friendship a visible part of her "brand." She was, as she'd said more than once, a girl's girl, and women's company was important to her. From her mother onward, she'd relied on women for guidance and comfort since childhood. From around the time of *Red*, she began socializing with women she met through her career and spending a good deal of time with them. Models, actresses, and musicians, they became known as the Squad, with Ed Sheeran the only prominent male Squaddie. Each Fourth of July from 2013 to 2016, Swift hosted a party for the Squad at Holiday House. The gatherings became synonymous with gorgeous, mainly thin, mainly white, young women frolicking in the Atlantic—numerous pictures found their way onto social media, especially from the 2016 party, the year Tom Hiddleston attended.

Sheeran, meanwhile, has cause to thank Swift for inviting him: it was at the 2015 party that he reconnected with Cherry Seaborn, now his wife. An old school friend, she was in Rhode Island that weekend and Sheeran asked Taylor if she could come to the bash. "The rest is history," Sheeran later told *People*. He and Seaborn had never completely lost touch, and during the North American leg of his 2015 *x* tour, at which point she was working in New York, they became texting buddies. But it wasn't until they met again at Swift's party that feelings developed. They married in December 2018.

It should be said here that Swift is also a solid supporter of younger female musicians, taking time to encourage and mentor them. When Dua Lipa was photographed wearing a *Speak Now* T-shirt at a soundcheck in Cologne in 2017, Swift's response was immediate and unequivocal. "I am SCREECHING WITH JOY!!!!!!" she wrote on Tumblr. She was also quick to send a kind text to singer-songwriter Lorde when the latter's second album, 2017's *Melodrama*, sold fewer copies in its first week than her debut, *Pure Heroine* (not by a huge amount—109,000 as opposed to

129,000—but it smarted). "I don't think first week record sales singularly define a legacy," Swift wrote, adding that she would forever picture Lorde in a rowboat with Annie Lennox, drifting along in a river of "cool cerebral ethereal dreams." The younger singer replied: "I love you so much for this." (Note: though Lorde and Lennox met at the 2016 Brit Awards, there's no evidence that the rowboat was anything other than a Swift figure of speech.)

Similarly, Olivia Rodrigo, who idolized both Swift and Lorde when she was finding her own feet as a singer and songwriter, has been on the receiving end of Swift's generosity. Now considered one of Gen Z's most bountifully talented stars, Rodrigo had just signed to Geffen Records in April 2020 when she sang Swift's "Cruel Summer" on MTV's *Alone Together Jam Session*. A track from the 2019 album *Lover*, "Cruel Summer" was a Swiftie favorite, so when Rodrigo posted the performance on her Instagram, fans took notice, and it filtered back to Swift herself. She posted Rodrigo's clip on her own Instagram and wrote: "THE TALENT. Love This!!! Thanks for this beautiful performance." A shocked Rodrigo replied: "TAYLOR SWIFT IS THE REASON I WRITE SONGS AND SHE POSTED ME ON HER STORY AND TOLD ME I WAS TALENTED???" On Twitter, she added: "I will never stop screaming."

There was more: Rodrigo's debut single, "drivers license," charted at No. 3 on iTunes on January 9, 2021, just behind a pair of tracks from the deluxe edition of *Evermore*, "It's Time to Go" and "Right Where You Left Me." Rodrigo's response: "Next to Taylor on the US iTunes chart I'm in a puddle of tears." Swift's answer to that was: "I say that's my baby and I'm really proud." As her own mother, Andrea, once used those words to describe Swift and they'd become a Swiftie catchphrase, there was a sense of Rodrigo being anointed heiress apparent.

A technical note: Rodrigo's debut album, *Sour*, gave Swift writing credits on the songs "Deja Vu" and "I Step Forward, 3 Steps Back"—not because Swift actively wrote them but because Rodrigo used the chords of Swift's "New Year's Day" on the latter and interpolated a section of "Cruel Summer" in the former. Sharing the credits with Swift and Swift's co-writers, Jack Antonoff and Annie "St. Vincent" Clark, also meant sharing substantial royalties.

Because of the Squad and the photogenic July Fourth parties, which were posted on Swift's Instagram for the public to enjoy, she found herself on the receiving end of much media snarkiness. Here she was, making a show of her friendships with supermodels and actresses, yet she'd spent her high school years as the class weird girl, perpetually snubbed by the cool girls. Critics had assumed that her experience of being shunned would keep her from ever joining an exclusive clique. She saw it rather differently. Still haunted by the memory of having to eat lunch alone because nobody wanted to sit with her, she was keen to celebrate the fact that she now had friends and to show them off to the world. There were no "mean girls" among them, they weren't victimizing anyone.

In 2019, looking back to the Squad backlash, she was rueful. She hadn't expected the negativity, she said, because she hadn't considered the optics. The Squad wasn't supposed to be a club that fans could only view from the outside; she thought spending time with her equally successful female friends was the equivalent of male artists and their "bro packs"—the patriarchy-approved way for men to bond and carouse. The Squad, as she saw it, was an inclusive group of counterparts—women at the top of their respective games.

In a March 2019 article for *Elle*, she reflected again on the Squad. "In my twenties I found myself surrounded by girls who wanted to be my friend. So I shouted it from the rooftops, posted pictures, and celebrated my newfound acceptance into a sisterhood, without realizing that other people might still feel the way I did when I felt so alone."

In the same piece, she also revealed the shocking cost of being an extremely successful young female artist. Since the 2017 Manchester Arena terrorist attack after an Ariana Grande concert and the mass-casualty shooting during a show by country singer Jason Aldean in Las Vegas the same year, Swift had been increasingly concerned about the safety of fans on her own tours. That was coupled with heightened vigilance about her own security. Her home addresses had been posted online, not just by "websites and tabloids," as she said, but by publications as benign as home-decor magazines—one had recently revealed that a $3 million dwelling "directly across" from one of Swift's places was available. The perceived level of intrusion had unnerved her, and she had begun to carry army-grade dressings made for gunshot or stab wounds. According to the manufacturer, they offer "a faster time to hemostasis" (clotting), which stems bleeding, and are recommended for use by hospitals, emergency responders, law enforcement, and the military. After sharing this sobering information, Swift stressed that she believed in the essential goodness of humanity. "We have to live bravely in order to truly feel alive," she wrote.

Back to the release of *Reputation*: as a start to an album era, "Look What You Made Me Do" took some beating. Written with Jack Antonoff, who also collaborated on five other tracks, it was industrial, stark, uncompromising. As *Reputation*'s lead single (and its most successful, reaching No. 1 in the US and the UK and selling 4 million copies by 2018), it completely rejigged the public's expectations of the new LP. It vied with the track that opens the album (and became its second single), "...Ready for It?," for the distinction of being the most dissonant thing on *Reputation* in a sonic sense. Electronic and glitchy, both songs broke new ground for her, and "...Ready for It?" even had her rapping (her flow had a touch of Nicki Minaj's peppiness).

Lyrically, though, they couldn't have been more different. "...Ready for It?," a co-write with Max Martin, Shellback, and Ali Payami (it was one of nine tracks Martin and Shellback co-wrote/produced), was about sexual desire, a subject Swift had rarely broached. In her Nashville days, she had written about passion, yearning, and cheating hearts, but her characters never went further than making out in the front seat of a pickup truck. Sex, as depicted in "Fifteen" from *Fearless*, stripped a girl of her power and was a route to heartbreak. As she went along, she cautiously introduced elements of erotic longing: "All Too Well" (*Red*) concerned itself with the misery of splitting up with someone who had emotionally possessed her; on "Wildest Dreams" (*1989*), she'd advanced to a boyfriend leaving his clothes around her bedroom.

But *Reputation* was the album on which Swift, who turned twenty-eight a month after it came out, finally reveled in eroticism. She's a sexual aggressor in "...Ready for It?," dreaming about what she and a man will do together; "Delicate" is one of her great descriptive songs—a whispery memory of a meeting in a bar on Manhattan's East Side that proceeded to a West Side apartment and a one-night stand. She shakily tells him that she wishes he were her boyfriend, a bravely vulnerable moment that lingers in the air because we never find out whether he returns her feelings. "Dress," meanwhile, is a straightforward lustathon—a slow jam with R&B cadences that mentions bedposts, removing her clothes, and wanting this man to be more than just a friend. The dress of the title was bought for the express purpose of taking it off—well, of course.

Despite the pure carnality of many of *Reputation*'s songs, it became known as a "revenge album" simply because the first song most people heard was "Look What You Made Me Do," in which she was implacably bent on getting her own back. ("I Did Something Bad," the album's third track, was equally vengeful— it exulted in taking down a foe, describing it as "fun"—but it wasn't a single, so it was less well-known to the wider public.) A hissing, clawing takedown of those she felt had orchestrated her fall from grace, "Look What" was sung in a vituperative whisper that was more unsettling than if she'd shouted. It was a shot across the bows, warning enemies that although they'd tried to bury her, she was back and out to settle scores.

But "Look What" was also striking for reasons beyond its cold rage. It contained an interpolation of Right Said Fred's 1991 dance-pop classic "I'm Too Sexy"—a track that couldn't have been further in tone from Swift's song but turned out to be an excellent fit thanks to its stentorian beat (the delighted disco trio tweeted "Thank you @taylorswift13 what a marvelous reinvention!"). More striking yet was another moment in the track—one that quickly became a meme, quoted by fans everywhere and analyzed in think pieces. Two minutes and fifty-six seconds into "Look What," Swift speaks into a landline receiver. All we see is her lips and right hand, the latter weighed down by silver-and-diamond snake rings. She informs the caller that, unfortunately, the former version of Taylor can't talk at the moment. Or ever, for that matter. Sorry, but she's dead.

That nine-second interlude was instantly recreated by hundreds of fans, who posted clips of themselves holding phones and speaking Swift's words. Debates broke out: did she mean she was no longer the eager-to-please nice girl—that she'd been toughened by the experience of being trolled by strangers who advised her that she was a snake and should quit music? Or was she mocking them? Or, as is likely, both?

When released, "Look What You Made Me Do" was streamed 84 million times in its first week and sold 350,000 copies—a colossal number in the streaming era. It became her fifth Hot 100 No. 1 in America and her first UK chart-topper. It paved the way for a big first week for *Reputation* when the album came out on November 10. On its first day, it sold 700,000 copies in the US; by the end of its debut week, it had racked up 1.2 million American sales, making her the first person ever to sell more than 1 million copies in the first weeks of four albums (*Speak Now, Red,* and *1989* were the others). It finished 2017 as the year's biggest seller and was also 2018's top seller. By July 2023, its total worldwide sales were 3.6 million— considerably lower than *1989*'s blockbusting 10.6 million, but *Reputation* had been a much more divisive record.

Some reviewers considered it one of her best releases; Slant, for instance, praised her "willingness to portray herself not as a victim, but the villain of her own story"—that was why the record was "such a fascinatingly thorny glimpse inside the mind of pop's reigning princess." Pitchfork highlighted its "bulletproof hooks and sticky turns of phrase." Most other reviewers found things to love. Some, however, didn't: *Now* thought its reliance on electronics sounded like she'd fabricated a release for "the club," while Consequence was unhappy about the R&B/hip-hop number "End Game," which featured the iconic rapper Future. His guest spot was fine, but Consequence was disappointed that the less iconic rapper Ed Sheeran was there too, spitting bars. (In fairness, Sheeran has always loved hip-hop and is highly esteemed by many rappers, including close friend Stormzy.)

Swift hadn't wanted *Reputation* to be viewed as a statement of rage. She explained her original intentions at a secret Chicago concert on June 27, 2018. Just 200 fans managed to get tickets for the show, which was sponsored by AT&T (she struck a deal with the communications giant in 2016 to provide special "performances and content"). The fans thought they'd won tickets for a party, until doors opened into a specially decorated small venue with a purpose-built stage; they'd had no idea that Swift would be performing.

Reputation had then been out for seven months and she was six weeks into the Reputation Stadium Tour, but by scheduling a small show during a gap between gigs in London and Louisville, Kentucky, Swift got a jolt of the up-close-and-personal fan interaction she loved. She told the crowd she had known from early on that the record would be called

Reputation and had built the album outward from there. "There were a lot of 'I'm angry at my reputation' moments [but other moments when I wondered,] 'What if my reputation makes a person I like not want to get to know me?'"

Despite the out-for-vengeance impression created by "Look What You Made Me Do," Swift saw *Reputation* as "an album about finding love throughout all the noise." She didn't mention Joe Alwyn at the concert, but she was eighteen months into a relationship with him. Her "reputation" hadn't stopped him getting to know her, and as the *Reputation* era came to an end, Swift was feeling good.

CHAPTER 12

Lover

My last album, *Reputation*, I really looked at that album," Swift told a small, invited audience in the summer of 2019. "I always do visuals and aesthetics in my mind of what an album represents. *Reputation* was, for me, a cityscape, nighttime, darkness—like full swamp-witch." She was in New York, hosting an event called Lover's Lounge—a fan gathering live streamed on YouTube Originals on August 22. It was the day before the release of *Lover*, and, as ever, Swift had wanted to convey the news in person. She was now thirteen years into her career—she made a point of saying so during the stream, because, as every Swiftie the world over knows, thirteen is her lucky number—and still saw fans as her friends. As such, she went to great lengths to arrange treats such as this; the evening included a performance and a special guest in the form of Stella McCartney. The two had collaborated on a clothing line, available from August 23 and priced at under $100 per item.

Lover's Lounge took place in a room filled with pink: from shag carpet and feathery cushions to the beanbags provided as audience seating, pastel pink was the color scheme. Complemented by a digitally created backdrop of drifting pink and lilac clouds, the room was as soft and wispy as the *Reputation* aesthetic had been hard-edged and dark.

Though Taylor had called *Reputation* "an album about finding love"—her words undoubtedly influenced by her happiness with Alwyn—she apparently revised her opinion along the way. At the Lover's Lounge, she looked back on it as her swamp-witch period; by December 2023, she was describing it to *Time* as "a goth-punk moment of female rage at being gaslit by an entire social structure." It's unclear whether the comment to *Time* pertained to the album itself or the segment of the Eras Tour devoted to it. She added: "I think a lot of people see it and [say], 'Sick snakes and strobe lights,'" which suggests she was referring to the stage set, rather than rewriting the history of the album. Certainly, her Eras performance of "Look What You Made Me Do" is a compact four minutes of churning fury (albeit leavened by humor, because it would be impossible not to smile when Karyn the Cobra makes her fang-flashing return to the stage—this time in CGI form rather than as a 63-foot inflatable, and backed up by four smaller cobras).

It's also plausible that her feelings about *Reputation* had changed because she and Alwyn went their separate ways early in 2023. It had been a landmark relationship for her: at six years, it was the longest she'd been with any boyfriend. They spent the COVID-19 pandemic together in London, during which he co-wrote (under the name William Bowery) two songs that would

Reputation marked a distinct style change for Swift, as she leaned into electropop and R&B. The album was written in response to the media scrutiny she received following *1989*'s success and has since been called one of the best albums of the 2010s.

MUELLER V. SWIFT

PUBLIC COURTROOM VIEWING ACCESS LINE

STARTS HERE 6AM

ABOVE: Swift takes great pride in using her powerful voice as a political tool. In 2017, she alleged that former DJ David Mueller had assaulted her, progressing to a weeklong court case in which she sought a symbolic $1 in damages. The jury found in Swift's favor, and she later revealed she'd pursued the case to empower other victims.

BELOW LEFT: Taylor performs at the 2019 VMAs, performing "You Need to Calm Down" and "Lover." She went on to win three awards, including Video of the Year.

BELOW RIGHT: As well as her supreme talent for singing and songwriting, Taylor has also turned her attention toward acting over the years. She starred in 2019's infamous *Cats* adaptation as Bombalurina, later saying, "I had a really great time working on that weird-ass movie."

LEFT: Taylor dated actor Joe Alwyn for six years from 2016 to 2023. Though many thought Alwyn would be Taylor's end-game partner, she cited personality differences as the reason for the split, later announcing *The Tortured Poets Department* in what many expected to be a direct takedown of Alwyn. *TTPD* proved to be a much more complex record, with many songs expressing her anger over her brief romance with The 1975 singer Matty Healy.

RIGHT: A thrilled Taylor accepts the Teen Choice Awards' Icon Award, thanking her fans and those behind the choice to feature her three cats—Benjamin Button, Olivia, and Meredith—on the surfboard trophy.

ABOVE: Captured on her phone, Taylor performs at the One World: Together at Home concert in April 2020, just as the coronavirus pandemic began to grip the world and the first lockdowns began.

BELOW: Following the surprise release of *Folklore* and *Evermore* in July and December 2020 respectively, Swift went on to win Album of the Year for *Folklore* at the 63rd Grammys—the first show to go ahead without an audience. Taylor went on to thank one of her socially distanced collaborators, Justin Vernon, saying, "I'm so excited to meet you someday."

ABOVE: May 2021 saw Swift be awarded the Global Icon Brit Award. She was the first woman and first non-British artist to receive the award, "in recognition of her immense impact on music across the world and incredible repertoire and achievements to date."

RIGHT: *Midnights* gave Taylor more opportunities to break records, this time becoming the only artist *ever* to win four Album of the Year Grammys.

ABOVE: *The Eras Tour* concert movie broke numerous records on release, becoming the highest grossing concert film of all time and earning more than $260 million, beating Michael Jackson's *This Is It*.

BELOW: Never short of collaborators to choose from, for the Eras Tour shows in California, Taylor was joined by Haim to sing their hit "No Body, No Crime." (*From left to right*): Este Haim, Taylor Swift, Danielle Haim, and Alana Haim.

ABOVE: The Eras Tour has been a wildly successful exercise in reinforcing Swift's connection with her fans, craftily tying together two decades of hits. The tour also marked her crossover into the title "billionaire."

RIGHT: Rumors surrounding Taylor and NFL player Travis Kelce began to circulate in autumn 2023. Since then, she has been spotted at numerous Kansas City Chiefs games, dancing in her seat and bringing an entirely new demographic to the game. As Kelce led the Chiefs to victory at Super Bowl LVIII, most news channels only had words for Taylor and her Swifties.

LEFT: The Swifties are widely considered responsible for Taylor's cultural influence—according to the *Washington Post*, they are "all part of one big friend group." Many Swifties have grown up with their icon's music, experiencing life alongside the singer and finding comfort and solace in her music.

The Eras Tour marks the culmination of two decades of passion and determination from Swift, highlighting her pride in her various reinventions over the years. Anyone who thought the tour signaled a last hurrah before a well-deserved break has been proven wrong already, as Taylor released her fifteenth studio album, *The Tortured Poets Department*, in early 2024. She shows no sign of slowing down anytime soon.

appear on 2020's *Folklore*—"Betty" and "Exile"—and three for *Evermore*—"Champagne Problems," "Coney Island," and the title track (on which he also played piano).

While the relationship was ongoing, they rarely talked about it other than in vague generalities. Even those were so infrequent that the media, and Swifties, had little to work with. In October 2018, while promoting the film *The Favourite*, a black comedy in which he played an eighteenth-century nobleman, Alwyn told *Vogue*: "I think we have been successfully very private and that has now sunk in for people . . . but I really prefer to talk about work." Swift, meanwhile, alluded to their romance in her 2020 documentary *Miss Americana*: "I was falling in love with someone who had a wonderfully normal, balanced life. We decided together we wanted our relationship to be private."

More power to them. Apparently, they lived an ordinary life in London, sharing Alwyn's flat in Crouch Hill, North London, then renting a bigger place in Primrose Hill and splurging mainly on Jo Malone Pomegranate Noir soap and Le Labo candles. Unsurprisingly, Alwyn inspired a clutch of songs on *Lover*, most notably "London Boy" and "Cornelia Street" (named after the downtown Manhattan street where she rented a townhouse in the early days of the relationship. The place became so associated with their romance that when they split up, some fans laid bouquets of flowers on the front steps).

The split was "announced" in early April 2023—not by the couple themselves but by the media; some outlets quoted a "source" who said: "Ultimately, they weren't the right fit for one another." Not being the right fit is the source of virtually all breakups, so there was nothing to be gleaned from that. In the absence of clarification from Swift and Alwyn, entertainment sites published retrospectives of the relationship, the most revealing of which was an *Us Weekly* feature titled, "Everything Taylor Swift and Joe Alwyn Have Said About Their Private Relationship." Really? *Everything?* Remarkably, the headline appeared to be true. In six years together, Swift and Alwyn had not only said almost nothing about their entwined lives, they'd rarely even referred to each other by name.

Rather than talking about their partnership, Alwyn would instead allude. During a panel discussion about the 2022 Hulu series *Conversations with Friends*, he was asked about playing a character who was in an open relationship, and his enticingly opaque reply was: "I think people can do what they want and makes them happy. I'm obviously happy in a monogamous relationship." So he couldn't be drawn on it, he quickly moved the discussion back to the show. In another *Conversations* interview, this time with *Extra*, he revealed that "she"—Swift— had read the Sally Rooney novel from which the series was adapted and "couldn't be a bigger fan of the project."

Swift, however, did occasionally mention Alwyn by name. "Joe and I really love sad songs. We've always bonded over music," she told Apple Music's Zane Lowe on December 12, 2020, during an interview about the just-released *Evermore* album. True enough: each of their *Folklore* and *Evermore* co-writes is downtempo and autumnal—as suitable as could be for two LPs conceived and recorded during a pandemic. She also named him, and gave a rare insight into his character, during *Folklore: The Long Pond Studio Sessions*, a concert film streamed on Disney+. "There's been a lot of discussion about William Bowery and his identity, because it's not a real person. So, William Bowery is Joe, as we know. He plays piano beautifully, and he's always just playing and making things up and kind of creating things," she said.

That, however, was as revealing as either of them ever got. Swift's relationship with Travis Kelce has been far more public, perhaps unavoidably. While neither party has discussed their mutual life as a couple, Swift has been a frequent and visible supporter when the Kansas City Chiefs play, and Kelce has traveled, sometimes thousands of miles, to attend Eras Tour shows. Their reaction to seeing one another after one of his games or one of her shows speaks volumes: the tactile Swift has met her match in Kelce, and a Traylor hug (as far as the internet is concerned, they're Traylor, just as she and Harry Styles were Haylor) can last a full three minutes. When the Chiefs won Super Bowl LVIII in February 2024, they locked themselves into a long embrace on the field that transmitted their joy at being together.

Again, though, she doesn't talk about it. The world wasn't even aware they were dating until September 24, 2023, when Swift attended a Kansas City Chiefs–Chicago Bears game at the Chiefs' home field, Arrowhead Stadium. (The Chiefs won, 41–10.) She was sharing a family box with Kelce's mother, Donna, and that was taken by many as confirmation that the two were a couple.

It's thought they met through a friend in the summer of 2023, after which Kelce went to her show, also at Arrowhead Stadium, when the Eras Tour came through Kansas City in July.

He'd hoped to give her his phone number but was thwarted by her habitually not speaking before or after shows in order to preserve her voice.

For some, ineluctable proof of their coupledom only came on November 11, when forty-three seconds of fan-filmed video footage from her show at Estadio River Plate in Buenos Aires was posted online. The fan's high-level seat had given them a view of the area just behind the stage, and they caught Swift coming offstage at the end of the gig. After a final wave at the crowd, she ran straight into the arms of the waiting Kelce. Arm in arm, they disappeared backstage, leaving a trace of stardust in their wake. It's hard to overstate how touching it was to witness their delight at being reunited—Kelce had the weekend off from his football commitments and had spent around thirteen hours on planes (assuming he used the shortest route, involving a change in Miami) to reach her.

He made an unusual choice for her; Swift has always been attracted to musicians and actors, whereas Kelce spends his professional life on the gridiron as a tight end—a position defined by *Diario AS* as "responsible for two things primarily—to catch passes from the quarterback and block for the running backs." He's one of the Chiefs' star players and was a critical figure in their triumphs in Super Bowl LIV and LVII. American sports pundit Pat McAfee characterizes him as "the greatest tight end in the history [of American football]."

But their different backgrounds could be the making of them, says super-Swiftie Tess Bohne, who has been live streaming the Eras concerts to 300,000 followers on TikTok. "Travis being a tight end [makes him] the perfect person for

Taylor," she told followers after the Buenos Aires footage emerged. It seems the reason is that tight ends can score touchdowns but can also step back and allow the quarterback to have the spotlight. "He is able to be a number one, but also knows when to step back and be a number two," Bohne said. In other words, while both halves of the couple are alphas, they don't compete with each other due to a tacit agreement that sometimes it will be Kelce's turn to shine, and sometimes Swift's.

And sometimes the spotlight is trained on both at the same time, such as in the moments following the Chiefs' victory against the San Francisco 49ers in Super Bowl LVIII on February 11, 2024. The game was, according to the BBC, seen by 123 million Americans, making it the most watched TV broadcast in the US since the *Apollo 11* moon landing in 1969. Swift's journey to see Kelce play was minutely followed by the media; she came straight from an Eras show at the Tokyo Dome, making a twelve-hour trip to Los Angeles via private jet, then traveling a further 270 miles to Las Vegas's Allegiant Stadium. CNN aired a clip of her performing in Tokyo just before she hurried to Haneda Airport for the flight; the Associated Press announced her arrival at Los Angeles International Airport at 3:30 p.m. on Saturday, the day before the game. Later, CBS News reported that she had safely reached her stadium suite in the company of Andrea Swift and friends Blake Lively and rapper Ice Spice. Flight-tracker apps made it possible to watch every moment of the flight from Haneda to LAX in real time, and the *Wall Street Journal* estimated that 20,000 people did exactly that.

Returning to *Lover*: Swift began writing it in the summer of 2018, during the Reputation Stadium Tour, and in July, she was seen at Manhattan's Electric Lady Studios. (Commissioned and part-funded by Jimi Hendrix in 1968, Electric Lady is as storied a recording studio as Abbey Road and has been the birthplace of some of rock and soul's most iconic recordings, including David Bowie's "Fame," Stevie Wonder's *Talking Book*, and Patti Smith's debut, *Horses*.) It's probable she recorded at least a few songs with Jack Antonoff, *Lover*'s main co-producer, during that summer, between Reputation shows, but the bulk of the recording took place after Reputation wrapped up on November 21.

(Note: Between December 2018 and April 2019, she also filmed the musical movie *Cats*, in which she played Bombalurina. Filming and recording overlapped by two months, making for a daunting schedule that would fell virtually every artist but Swift, who's energized by an overflowing work schedule. "Beautiful Ghosts," co-written for the film with Andrew Lloyd Webber, received Grammy and Golden Globe nominations.)

Recording for *Lover* finished on February 24, 2019, signaled that day by an Instagram post. It was a print of palm trees under a washed-blue sky spangled with stars, above a caption showing seven palm-tree emojis. It didn't take much Easter-egg hunting to work out that her seventh album was on its way. It was still six months away, and its lead single, "Me!," wasn't due until April 26, but the palm trees conveyed a broad picture of what was to come. The trees were a palate cleanser, eradicating the taste of *Reputation* and implying that the new era was to be a light, happy one. In the Lover's Lounge broadcast in August, Swift said exactly that. "*Lover* is something that I'm so proud of ... because it's a natural continuation of a story in my life, the way that events have unfolded. But this album felt aesthetically very daytime, very sunlit fields. I wrote music from a much more open, free, romantic, whimsical place."

Highly observant fans would have picked up an early clue from a "vertical video" (which was separate from the "official" video) for *Reputation*'s penultimate single, "Delicate." The vertical clip was only watchable on Spotify, and the pertinent thing was that she had polished her nails in a variety of pastel shades. They're not easy to spot, but at two minutes and fifty-six seconds, they're plainly visible as she pushes her outstretched fingers toward the camera. Clearly, she wants them to be noted, and once *Lover* and its watercolor hues came along, everyone knew why.

So her seventh album was happy, garlanded in the contentment that comes from being in love with someone who loves you back. In her online foreword, she called it "a love letter to love itself . . . We are what we love." "Me!" was her bubbliest single in years, a froth of bouncy affirmations addressed to herself and Alwyn, and to her fans. To Alwyn, the song unapologetically says that, despite being hard work at times, Swift was still very much worth it because there was nobody else like her. To fans, she counseled the joy of being true to themselves, sending the message home with a one-word chorus: "Me-ee-ee, me-ee-ee!" She extended each "me" to three syllables, making it plain that it really was all about her-er-er. There was no hidden code; Swift was simply promising that being "me" was the road to fulfillment.

Sharing vocals with Brendon Urie, then leader of Panic! At The Disco (he dissolved the band in 2023), she was in full vibrant effect, a mood emphasized by the song's remarkable video. It starts with a pink-and-white snake slithering across pastel cobblestones before facing the camera and opening its mouth to a fearsome extent. Its tongue flickers menacingly, then the creature spits out . . . pastel butterflies. *Reputation* is dead; long live *Lover*.

The rest of the video is a fever dream of angels, unicorn battlements, Urie floating through the sky holding an open umbrella . . . image after fantastical image until the two singers exit stage right as the skirt of Swift's blue ballgown turns into iridescent liquid, spilling onto the cobblestones behind her. *Variety*'s description of it as a "phantasmagorical delight" accurately summed it up.

Dueting with Urie wasn't a capricious decision. Swift had loved Panic! At The Disco since her schooldays, when she and Abigail Anderson drove around Hendersonville, shouting along to their 2006 signature song, "I Write Sins Not Tragedies." (Their appreciation might have been helped along by Urie being an emo heartthrob.) For his own part, Urie had always been a Swift fan; he had told PopCrush as early as 2014: "T-Swift, honestly from the get-go I was into that girl. She's super talented, really smart songwriter, really fun. She seems like really fun to work with."

In January 2019, she texted him with an idea for a song. "I wrote back," he told broadcaster Zach Sang a few months later. "I am such a big fan, I just basically gushed over her: 'I love you, I've loved you for years.'" She told him she didn't yet have a bridge for the song—could he write one? On the day they were booked to record, he woke with a 104-degree fever.

He had already composed the bridge in his head but, woozy and feverish, was worried he'd forget it. He sang it onto a voicenote, hurried to the studio, and he and Swift managed to record "Me!" there and then. "She's so kind about everything," he reminisced, still a bit dazzled. What impressed him most? "Her passion for it. I thought I had a passion, I thought I was a hard worker, that I was ambitious—she gets behind her ideas a hundred percent. When she's feeling something, she feels that idea and it is gorgeous. The coolest thing to witness firsthand."

The release of "Me!" was an important evolutionary step for Swift as a mature artist because it was the first song to which she'd ever owned the rights. Reviews, however, were mixed. It was so fluffy, so bright, so pastel that critics either loved it or hated it. It was "a cloyingly goofy Disney-pop confection" (The Ringer) or "a totally canonical Taylor Lead Single" (*Rolling Stone*), with little middle ground. As her first new music in more than a year it was destined to be commercially successful, and so it was: it zipped to No. 2 in its second week on the *Billboard* Hot 100, and if Lil Nas X's record-breaking "Old Town Road" hadn't just started its nineteen-week run at No. 1, "Me!" almost certainly would have been Swift's sixth chart-topping single.

One song on the album had been especially difficult to write. The gentle, piano-led ballad "Soon You'll Get Better" came about when Andrea Swift's breast cancer, diagnosed in 2015, returned in 2019. Taylor's childhood idols, The Chicks, provided vocal harmonies as Swift softly sang about the doctor's office, her prayers, and the impossibility of facing life without her mother. The family had coped with the disease before; in the mid-2000s, Scott Swift had had prostate cancer and made a relatively quick recovery. Andrea's illness was more tenacious. The decision to put the song on *Lover* was taken by the whole family, "and [the song is] something I'm so proud of, but it's just really hard . . . to emotionally deal with that song," she said during her August 22 Lover's Lounge live stream.

Wanting to spend as much time as possible with her mother meant that a globe-circling stadium tour of the album was out of the question. Instead, when she did tour *Lover*, she intended to visit just fourteen cities—a manageable number, with gaps between shows that would provide ample time to see Andrea. Because of coronavirus, however, the tour never happened (the cancellation is discussed later in this chapter).

Lover's biggest fan favorite—defined as a track adored by Swifties above and beyond their feelings for the LP's other tracks—was "Cruel Summer." A bubbling new-wave song co-written by Annie "St. Vincent" Clark (Jack Antonoff and Clark had apparently worked on part of the instrumentation for St. Vincent's *Masseduction* album, found it didn't fit and repurposed it for "Cruel Summer"), it explored classic romantic territory. Its subject was a "fever dream" of a night; she'd spent it with—seemingly—someone who wasn't her boyfriend but soon would be, and she was wracked with guilt and confusion. Some fans guessed—unconfirmed by Swift—that it set out her conflict of emotions regarding Alwyn, whom she had met and fancied, and Hiddleston, whom she was dating.

It was set to become a single in the summer of 2020, timed to tie in with the Lover Fest tour. Despite that plan being scuppered by COVID-19, "Cruel Summer" never went away. Its streaming numbers remained steady, even after the *Lover* era finished and Swift released her next three albums (*Folklore* and *Evermore* in 2020 and *Midnights* in 2022). Then it had a prominent place on the Eras Tour setlist as the second song played every night, and the numbers rose again. What could Swift do but finally make it a single? Out on June 13, 2023, it reached No. 1 on the Hot 100 on October 23.

Then there was "Miss Americana & the Heartbreak Prince," a *Lover* track that had no Swiftian precedent. "This song is about disillusionment with our crazy world of politics and inequality, set in a metaphorical high school," she wrote in a note shown onscreen during *Love, Taylor: Lover Enhanced Album*—a partnership with Spotify that ran for several days before *Lover* was released. It included yet-to-be-heard *Lover* lyrics, audio, and written messages about the songs and several of her favorite love songs by other artists, including Nicki Minaj's "Come See About Me" and Blondie's "Maria."

Nobody had expected Swift to express political views. Along with most country singers, she never touched on the subject in her Nashville days or even after she transitioned to pop. It was too divisive, and she'd grown accustomed to swerving interview questions about who she supported in the 2016 presidential election—the one that brought Donald Trump to the White House—or how she felt about the Black Lives Matter movement and her views on reproductive rights. The nearest she had come to taking a public stand was a line in "Welcome to New York" on *1989* that declared support for LGBTQ+ rights. "Miss Americana" was an upbeat, synthpop corrective to her years of near-silence.

Though the "metaphorical high school" of the lyric doesn't allow for straightforward politicizing, Swift uses images like a torn prom dress and a losing football team to convey her thoughts. Perhaps she'd been galvanized by a previous brush with politics before the US midterm elections of 2018, when she'd dipped a toe into the water with a lengthy Instagram post that began, "In the past I've been reluctant to publicly voice my political views." It condemned systemic racism, homophobia, and misogyny in America and announced that she would vote for the Democratic candidates for the Senate and House of Representatives. Swift posted it on October 7, urging young Americans to register to vote by October 9, the day registration closed in the state of Tennessee. Within two days, 102,000 people did. Trump's response: "Let's say I like Taylor's music about 25 percent less now."

So "Miss Americana" was her first musical state-of-the-union message, and it also lent its name to a documentary that launched in January 2020. Where "Miss Americana" the song had alluded and implied, *Miss Americana* the Netflix documentary came right out and said, vehemently. The 85-minute film was a truly eye-opening capture of a year of her life, from the Reputation Stadium Tour through the recording and release of *Lover.* Its director, Lana Wilson, said: "I see the movie as looking at the flip side of being America's sweetheart."

Obviously, America's sweetheart had toughened up since the Kardashian/West pile-on—she even sequenced *Lover* to start with a track that appears to speak directly to them, "I Forgot That You Existed." To go by the lyric, she hasn't forgotten at all, but has instead achieved a state of indifference and can no longer be hurt by them. But it took a year out of the spotlight and endless reflection to arrive at this Zen state.

What *Miss Americana* examines is her evolution—her "good little girl" starting point to an adulthood that has empowered her and made her unafraid of not being good. She had grown up subscribing to a "complete and total belief system" that foregrounded "a need to be thought of as good . . . the main thing that I always tried to be was . . . a good little girl." The trailer for the film, which premiered at the Sundance Film Festival in Park City, Utah, on January 23, 2020, promised that it would be "beyond everything you think you know." That it was.

Swift spoke for the first time about the disordered eating that had ruled her life for several years as she struggled to stay a size 00—the size she thought was necessary to meet the public's expectations of a pop star. It was a constant trade-off: if she gained enough weight to have the curvaceous "ass that everybody wants," her stomach wasn't flat, and vice versa. She'd undergone periods of starving herself, resulting in feeling as if she would pass out onstage. She had finally overcome the impulse, she said, by accepting that her body wasn't designed for extreme thinness. She was now a size 6 and felt the difference in her energy levels—she could do a show and not feel depleted.

She was also adamant that it was time for her to take a political stance in public. In one of the film's most talked-about scenes, she tells her team that she feels compelled to speak out about her voting intentions in the upcoming midterms (see earlier paragraph). Her father and management team, much opposed to her plan, try everything in their power to dissuade her. One warns that her concert audiences will halve overnight. Someone else asks whether Bob Hope or Bing Crosby (who died in 2003 and 1977, respectively) had ever told fans how to vote (she could have countered with the fact that Frank Sinatra had vocally supported John F. Kennedy's 1960 presidential campaign, even re-recording one of his hits, "High Hopes," with a new pro-JFK lyric).

The same person asks whether Mick Jagger had ever done it (no, Jagger has never endorsed a particular candidate, but he did co-write "Street Fighting Man," one of the most enduring anti–Vietnam War/pro-revolution anthems of the 1960s counterculture). Someone else warns her that making a pro-Democrat stand could put her at risk: "Just from a security viewpoint: 'Taylor Swift comes out against Trump.'"

She replies fiercely: "I don't care if they write that!" She wishes she'd come out against him in 2016, she adds. What was most important to her right then, in October 2018, was being "on the right side of history." Scott Swift reminds her that he's so concerned for her safety that he's bought armored cars.

Taylor tearfully retorts that Tennessee's Republican candidate for the Senate, a woman, had voted against the reauthorizing of the federal Violence Against Women Act, "which is basically protecting us against domestic abuse and stalking." She points at herself. "Stalking!" As the subject of much unwanted attention, the word has great resonance for her. She asks Scott to forgive her for doing it—in other words, for the Instagram post she was about to put online—but she was doing it anyway.

Miss Americana also looks at subjects that were already in the public domain, such as the sexual assault backstage in Denver in 2013 and subsequent defamation lawsuit, and frames them in a new way. Swift reveals, for example, that winning the lawsuit and receiving the $1 damages she had requested gave her no sense of "victory." The process had been "dehumanizing"; though there was evidence that the assault had happened— along with a photograph, she had witnesses—she'd had to relive the moment in court. (Note: The plaintiff paid his $1 damages in the form of a gold dollar coin embossed with the head and shoulders of the Native American woman Sacagawea. For reasons unexplained, he called the coin a "jab" at Swift.) The case was a turning point—from there, she felt impelled to use her platform to advocate for others.

Miss Americana's reviews were widely positive. A few inexplicably complained that she'd broken no new ground, but many more found it, as the *Salt Lake Tribune* did, "an eye-opening look at Taylor Swift finding a new voice."

Returning to *Lover*'s release in August 2019, it surprised no one when it opened at No. 1 in the US. It was her sixth album to top the American chart and her fourth in the UK. Extraordinarily, in its week of release, its sales were greater than the combined total of the other 199 albums in the American Top 200. To put it another way, purchases of *Lover* made up 27 percent of all album sales that week. Though its 867,000 opening-week sales were lower than *Reputation*'s 1.2 million, they were still higher than any other LP managed in its debut week in 2019. By December, it had sold 1.085 million physical/ digital copies, making it 2019's biggest-selling album in America.

But the *Lover* era was marked by headline-making events that overshadowed the album itself. First: coronavirus, which made it impossible to tour the LP. In September 2019, she'd announced dates for Lover Fest, scheduled to take place in summer 2020. Swift was set to play seventeen concerts in fourteen cities, mainly in Europe, and planned to add more UK dates to the two already on the itinerary (Hyde Park in London and the Glastonbury Festival). This would have been her first Glastonbury show—a highly desirable gig to have landed because of the festival's prestige and the sense that a show there is an accolade that has to be earned. In April 2020, she postponed the shows until 2021, and in February 2021, with no clear idea of when live music would return, she canceled the tour altogether. She didn't tour again until Eras.

Second: her Big Machine contract ended. She had fulfilled the terms of the deal, which were to make six albums, and when promotional activities for the sixth, *Reputation*, ended in November 2018, she was officially a free agent. Thus, *Lover* was her first album to appear on a label other than Big Machine. As of November 19, her new company was Republic Records, a subsidiary of Universal Music Group.

When she signed to Big Machine at fifteen, she had, as was customary, given the label the rights to her albums in return for a cash advance. Why would she hand them over? Because Scott Borchetta had experience and clout—attributes that were vital to a teenager looking to get her career out of the starting gate. She'd spent most of 2004 pleading with RCA to escalate her development deal to the next level, where she would be a signed recording artist, allowed to make her first album. So being offered a contract with Big Machine that stipulated that the label would release and promote six albums in return for the rights to the master recordings would have seemed an enticing deal in 2004. As talented as Scott Borchetta thought she was, he was still taking a gamble; there was no guarantee whatsoever that Big Machine would recoup its investment.

The gamble turned out to be the canniest he had ever taken. By August 2018, according to *Billboard*, her sales and streams comprised 34 percent of Big Machine's market share. The same month, *Variety* reported that her music made up a much bigger share than that—according to a source close to Big Machine, some years the percentage was closer to eighty.

What is important to note here is that Big Machine had the rights to the masters of Swift's first six albums (masters are the original recordings, and ownership is valuable because it provides an income from sales and streams). However, as Swift had written the songs, they could not be *licensed* without her permission for use in other mediums, such as films or ads. So if the master owner received a "synch" request to use a Swift track in a TV series, Swift, as songwriter, could refuse permission. In December 2019, she revealed that her team received "a dozen" synch enquiries every week—and declined all of them because she only wanted her recordings used if she owned them.

Having said that—it's complicated—any of her songs could be covered by another singer and the cover version used in that same TV series, as long as they got a license from the owner of the composition, who is Swift. Seemingly, it's easier, and cheaper, to obtain a cover license than a license to use the original version. An example is "Bad Blood," which featured in the animated Netflix series *Big Mouth* in October 2019, sung by Kina Grannis and CLARA. There was also a dark, slowed-down cover of "Look What You Made Me Do," credited to Jack Leopards & The Dolphin Club, that featured on the TV series *Killing Eve* on May 24, 2020. Significantly, had Swift not written her own material, she wouldn't have been able to re-record it; the *Taylor's Version*s would never have happened.

Swift was especially excited about the *Killing Eve* feature, tweeting on May 25: "VERY STOKED about this cover of lwymmd on @KillingEve by Jack leopards & the dolphin club!!" Swifties got on the case instantly and uncovered facts that pointed toward Swift herself: it was produced by Jack Antonoff and Nils Sjöberg—the pseudonym she used to co-write Calvin Harris's "This Is What You Came For"—the track's artwork was a doctored photo of her brother Austin as a child, and Austin had formerly used the name "The Dolphin Club" on Twitter. A fan going by the name stillhavehope99 commented on Reddit: "This is really cool. Taylor meets Johnny Cash. Also . . . what a power move." But how was it a power move? An explanation was offered by *Paper* magazine: "Why would Swift start a fake band to release versions of her old music? So she could get the song on TV without Braun earning a cent." Music manager Scooter Braun had by May 2020 bought Big Machine, which is covered at the end of this chapter.

Big Machine began negotiations to renew her contract months in advance. Swift's position was clear from the outset: she would only renew if the rights to her music reverted to her. According to Swift, the label offered to return one master recording for every new album Swift made, up to six albums. Faced with the prospect of being tied to the label for around ten more years, she began to field offers from other companies.

Perhaps relevant to her decision was talk around Nashville that for the last few years Borchetta had been thinking of selling Big Machine. His problem: without the rights to Swift's music, the label would lose much of its value.

In the event, on November 19, 2018, Universal Music Group announced: "Taylor Swift, one of the music industry's most creatively and commercially successful artists in history, signed a global recording agreement with Universal Music Group (UMG), the world leader in music-based entertainment. The multi-album agreement, effective immediately, deepens the relationship between Swift and UMG [UMG was Big Machine's distributor] and builds upon the enormous success she achieved with Big Machine Records."

On the same day, Swift released her own statement, via Tumblr: "I'm ecstatic to announce that my musical home will be Republic Records and Universal Music Group. Over the years, [UMG Chairman] Sir Lucian Grainge and [Republic Records CEO] Monte Lipman have been such incredible partners. It's also incredibly exciting to know that I'll own all of my master recordings that I make from now on."

Her contract also contained an undertaking by UMG that, should the company sell its shares in Spotify (the streaming platform had floated under the name Spotify Technology SA on the New York Stock Exchange in April 2018), they would pay some of the cash to its artists. "There was one condition that meant more to me than any other deal point," she wrote. "I asked that any sale of their Spotify shares result in a distribution of money to their artists, non-recoupable. They have generously agreed to this."

"Non-recoupable" makes a big difference here. Swift persuaded UMG to share any Spotify profits, but many signed acts owe their label money because they haven't yet earned enough to pay back their advances. Swift's intention was that any Spotify money be paid directly to artists, rather than toward reducing the money they owed to UMG. If, hypothetically, an act owed UMG $100,000 and their portion of any Spotify share proceeds came to $25,000, the label would be within its rights to apply the $25,000 to the unrecouped balance. That would reduce the artist's debt to $75,000, but they were still a long way from paying it off. What UMG promised to do, thanks to Swift, was to put the $25,000 straight into the artist's bank account, where it would be a much-welcomed boost.

At the end of her statement, she added: "I want to express my heartfelt thanks to Scott Borchetta for believing in me as a fourteen-year-old and for guiding me through over a decade of work that I will always be so proud of."

The next time she publicly mentioned Borchetta, her language would be less temperate. On June 30, 2019, Borchetta and Scooter Braun jointly announced that Braun had bought Big Machine. The price paid by Braun, later revealed to be $330 million, wasn't mentioned. "The idea of Scott and I working together is nothing new, we've been talking about it since the beginning of our friendship," Braun said. "He's built a brilliant company full of iconic songs and artists. Who wouldn't want to be a part of that?"

Borchetta added: "Scooter and I have been aligned with 'big vision brings big results' from the very first time we met in 2010. Since then I have watched him build an incredible and diverse company that is a perfect complement to the Big Machine Label Group. Our artist-first spirit and combined roster of talent, executives, and assets is now a global force to be reckoned with."

Swift replied in a lengthy post on Tumblr, which said, in part: "This is my worst-case scenario. This is what happens when you sign a deal at fifteen to someone for whom the term 'loyalty' is clearly just a contractual concept. When I left my masters in Scott's hands, I made peace with the fact that eventually he would sell them. Never in my worst nightmares did I imagine the buyer would be Scooter."

Swift's shock at the sale resounded through her world. The origins of her falling-out with Scooter Braun are difficult to pinpoint; in the Tumblr post, she referred to "the incessant, manipulative bullying I've received at his hands for years," and provided as an example Kim Kardashian's leaking of the 2016 phone conversation with Kanye West. Kardashian and West were Braun management clients, and Taylor claimed Braun had encouraged them to harass her online. (Note: Braun and West ended their working relationship in 2018.) She also implied that another Braun client, Justin Bieber, had joined in—in 2016, Bieber had posted a picture of himself on a video call with West and Braun and captioned it: "Taylor swift what up."

Bieber—who had become a pop icon since Braun discovered him on YouTube in 2008, when the then fourteen-year-old was posting videos of himself covering R&B hits—apologized after he saw Taylor's Tumblr post. Writing on Instagram the same day, June 30, he explained that he'd thought the video-call photo and "What up" caption funny at the time and that Braun hadn't been involved. In fact, Braun had told him not to joke about it. Braun "has had [Swift's] back" since 2009, he said, when Bieber supported her on some Fearless Tour dates. Bieber was now dismayed by Swift's claim that Braun had bullied her. "One thing i know is both scooter and i love you," he wrote, and urged her to contact Braun to resolve "any feelings that need to be addressed."

As Swift tried to process the Big Machine sale—technically, the acquisition was between Big Machine Label Group and Braun's company, Ithaca Holdings LLC—singer Kelly Clarkson offered advice that would see Swift launch a project so bold that it realigned her career. Rather than being viewed as merely an icon, she would be lauded for taking control of the situation and turning it entirely to her advantage. "Just a thought," Clarkson tweeted on July 13. "U should go in & re-record all the songs that U don't own the masters on exactly how U did them but put brand new art & some kind of incentive so fans will no longer buy the old versions."

While this was happening, Swift was, it hardly needs saying, engrossed in the rollout of Lover. "Me!" had been followed on June 14 by second single "You Need to Calm Down," and on the day news of the Big Machine sale broke, the release of Lover was eight weeks away. The BMLG announcement could hardly have come at a trickier time, but Swift thrives on challenge in a way that's alien to mere mortals. She had always known that she was contractually allowed to re-record her music after a certain amount of time had passed—many record deals include the same permission, imposing a waiting period of two years after a contract expires, or five years after an album's release. In

Swift's case, it meant that if she wanted to, she could start re-recording the earliest albums in November 2020.

It's entirely possible that was what she planned to do from the moment she found out about the sale. However, Clarkson's suggestion is popularly seen as the motivating factor. Clarkson also said that she would make a point of buying any re-recordings, and many fans spoke up after that, saying they would do the same. Their enthusiasm for the idea was tantamount to a poll, assuring Swift and her team that if she remade the albums, they would sell. And on August 22 came the first announcement of her intentions: interviewed on CBS News' *Sunday Morning*, she was asked if she might re-record. "*Oh, yeah*," she said, with what could only be described as jubilation. Later that day, she revealed more on *Good Morning America*: "It's something that I'm very excited about doing because my contract says that starting November 2020 . . . I can record albums one to five all over again. I'm very excited about it."

It's scant exaggeration to say that quite a few people were excited: Swift, her fans, other artists—who would be watching and learning—and much of the music industry, for whom the *Taylor's Version* project (as it wasn't yet known) served as a reminder to pore over re-recording clauses in artist contracts.

CHAPTER 13

Folklore and Evermore

Folklore and *Evermore*, released in July and December 2020, respectively, were the albums nobody was expecting. They appeared with no fanfare except notices on Instagram and Twitter the day before release, and they remain unique efforts—the outliers of Swift's catalogue. They explore entirely different musical terrain from anything she'd done before, and do so without the gradual transition effected by *Red*, which sprinkled pop songs among the country in preparation for Swift's move to full pop on *1989*.

Folklore—to consider them in turn—is her indie/folk/alt-rock record: sixteen tracks of spare, intimate minimalism. The mood is wistful but light—Swift considered it to represent spring and summer. The darker, melancholic *Evermore* is autumn and winter. Both are manifestations of a place in her mind that she calls "the folklorian woods." She used that term in a tweet: "it feels like we were standing on the edge of the folklorian woods and had a choice: to turn and go back or to travel further into the forest of this music." Posted on December 10, 2020, it was the first public notice that *Folklore*'s "sister album," *Evermore*, would arrive at midnight that night.

If *Evermore* is sometimes the near-forgotten sister, it can only blame *Folklore*'s singularity, which grabbed all the attention. It invented a world of fictional characters—a development fostered by Swift's deciding that she had gone as far as she could, at least for the moment, with her "diaristic" writing style. There were still some autobiographical tracks, such as the gothically haunted "My Tears Ricochet," a betrayed, resentful recounting of a conflict between her and "the person who was your best friend [and] is now your biggest nemesis," as she told *Entertainment Weekly*. That description was taken to mean that it was about Scott Borchetta; if it was, he must have felt scorched by the lyric. The language stung: he had "buried" her, "killed" her, was "cursing" her.

Other tracks, however, were pure fiction. "The Last Great American Dynasty," for one, was inspired by the life of Rebekah Harkness, the oil heiress who once owned Holiday House in Rhode Island. The song, an alt-rock shuffle, was a sly put-down of Rhode Island high society of the mid-twentieth century— specifically, the "pearl-clutching" worthies who found Harkness's anarchic "Bitch Pack" spirit a threat to morals. Harkness was known to friends as Betty, so it's tempting to think she might also have influenced the track "Betty"—*Folklore*'s third single. On the other hand, the fictional "Betty" in the song is enmeshed in what Swift called "a teenage love triangle," and the other points of the triangle are called James and Inez. Swift's close friend Blake Lively happens to have children named Betty, James, and

Inez, so that appears to be conclusive proof of where the name came from—though it would be lovely to think that something of Betty Harkness's wild heart exists in the lonesome, harmonica-laced Americana of "Betty."

The lyric, told from the viewpoint of seventeen-year-old James, mentions Betty's cardigan—an unglamorous, everyday garment that's the subject of its own song. "Cardigan" was the album's first single (and only No. 1) and is much loved to this day. Swift was thirty when she wrote it, but her evocation of high school innocence is unexpectedly pure. Her whispery vocal—reminiscent of Lana Del Rey if Del Rey's cynicism had been stripped from her voice—shimmers; in this one, she's Betty, singing about James putting her on like the sweater he shoves under the bed.

It wasn't just the quality of the songs that made *Folklore* such a hit. It ticked hitherto nonexistent boxes. Nobody knew they needed this low-key, rustic-leaning album until it actually arrived: only then, while quarantined people were wondering what to do with themselves during the first pandemic summer, did it become obvious that here was an album made for this precise situation. It wasn't intrusive; it just provided company. *NME* wrote: "*Folklore* feels like Swift has traveled to a metaphorical cabin in the woods and concocted a gorgeous, relaxed record filled with modern folk songs."

There was another attraction: she made most of the album with Aaron Dessner from the revered indie band The National, and he brought the equally admired Wisconsin-based singer-songwriter Justin Vernon with him. Vernon, who records under the name Bon Iver (pronounced "bone-eevare"), had collaborated with Dessner under the name Big Red Machine and here duetted with Swift on the track "Exile." His oak-aged voice was an atmospheric counterpoint to her misty, Appalachian-sounding delivery. *Folklore's* second single, it reached No. 6 in the US and 8 in Britain.

It brought in an audience that had never had much time for Swift before because of her pop leanings. *Folklore* swung the focus away from *Lover's* glitz and trained it on her songwriting, and these new listeners discovered that there was a good deal more to her than they'd assumed. "All those fifty-year-old men who dismissed her were forced to admit how good she was," Dave Fawbert told the *Guardian* (as mentioned earlier, his UK-wide club night, Swiftogeddon, founded in 2019, plays only Swift songs).

Since May 2019, Swift had been listening repeatedly to *I Am Easy to Find*, the album released that month by The National. When America went into lockdown in the spring of 2020, Swift kept playing it (and also found herself reading more than she'd ever read and watching more films than ever before). She got the idea of contacting Dessner, The National's guitarist/keyboardist/ co-writer, to gauge his interest in collaborating on an album. He was interested enough to send a hard drive of ideas he'd been working on. She sent back lyrics and vocals the same day.

Recording remotely, they fashioned nine of *Folklore's* sixteen songs; Swift made the rest with Jack Antonoff, Joe Alwyn, or—on "Betty"—a committee composed of herself, Dessner, Antonoff, *and* Alwyn. It entered the *Billboard* Top 200 at No. 1 and remained there for eight weeks, becoming the top seller of 2020. In March 2021, it won the Grammy for Album of the Year—her third win in the category.

The second half of 2020, post-*Folklore*, saw three major developments. In November, two years after the Big Machine contract had expired, she began her re-recording program. The first she tackled wasn't the debut but its 2008 follow-up *Fearless*, her first American No. 1 and her first Album of the Year Grammy winner. As of spring 2024, the debut has yet to be remade, and theories abound about its absence, with many suggestions pointing to *Taylor Swift*'s comparatively low streaming numbers—it's been said that the debut accounts for only 1.25 percent of all of her album streams. With the *Taylor's Version*s, she was going where no pop colossus had gone before, and it probably made more strategic sense to launch with the LP that brought her to national prominence than with a record that wouldn't get the same attention and sales. Swift had also been open about wanting to license her music for films and TV, and *Fearless* had several of the most-wanted potential synchs, particularly "Love Story" and "White Horse."

On November 16, 2020, it was announced that Scooter Braun had sold Swift's masters and all recording rights to a company called Shamrock Capital. The sale price was said to have been in the area of $405 million. Swift was now free of many business ties to the earlier years of her career, including Sony/ATV Publishing. In February 2020, the contract she had signed as a fourteen-year-old expired, and she moved on to Universal Music Publishing Group.

As the first quarantine year approached its end, Swift pulled a third rabbit out of her hat. On December 10, she posted a new photo on Instagram: the back of her head and shoulders, with her hair arranged into an untidy braid and her body enveloped by a rough, outdoorsy plaid jacket. The ensemble was perfect for tramping across bare winter fields like the one shown in the picture. It was the first time she'd ever turned her back to the camera on an album cover—for that was what this picture was: the cover of her next album. By the picture alone, it seemed that Swift's exploration of rustic pathways and "folklorian woods" hadn't yet ended.

And, fashion being what it is, *Stylist* magazine published a guide to recreating her hairstyle. "A loose soft French braid like this keeps hair tamed whilst looking stylish," said Adam Reed, UK editorial ambassador for L'Oréal Professionnel. He suggested "prepping with a salt spray" for extra grip and revealed that "the key to Taylor's braid is not to overthink it; it's fine for some pieces to be bigger than others."

Under the picture on Instagram, Swift wrote: "I'm elated to tell you that my ninth studio album, and folklore's sister record, will be out tonight at midnight eastern. It's called evermore." As with *Folklore*, she had provided less than twenty-four hours" notice. "To put it plainly, we just couldn't stop writing songs," she continued, explaining that her co-creators were, as before, Dessner, Antonoff, Justin Vernon, and "WB" (William Bowery/Joe Alwyn), and a few new faces had joined in. These turned out to be her close friends Este, Danielle, and Alana Haim—aka the band Haim—and Dessner's group, The National. Collaborating with Swift for the first time, Haim harmonized on the quietly menacing "murder ballad" "No Body, No Crime," while National vocalist Matt Berninger duetted with Swift on the desolate breakup track "Coney Island." Located in Brooklyn, the borough where The National formed, Coney Island is a seaside amusement area that flourishes in summer, but the song is set in the wintry offseason, making the blend of Berninger's and Swift's voices surpassingly atmospheric.

"I loved the escapism I found in [*Folklore*'s] imaginary/ not imaginary tales," she wrote in the Instagram caption— and that was the reason she was now releasing *Folklore*'s sister. She also hoped it would provide consolation to the many who would be celebrating the holiday season alone due to COVID-19 isolation rules. The December 10 announcement fell on the birthday of Emily Dickinson, the nineteenth-century Massachusetts poet who has grown in stature since her death to become a towering figure of American literature. (It doesn't need saying that Swift's own birthday was three days later; she turned thirty-one on December 13.)

The singer, who later discovered that she was distantly related to Dickinson, was a great admirer and possibly found inspiration for the new album's name in Dickinson's 1858 poem "One Sister Have I in Our House," which ends "Sue— forevermore!" *Evermore*'s meditative, folky tenth track, "Ivy," has been interpreted as a love song from Dickinson to Sue—her sister-in-law Susan Gilbert—with whom she is assumed (but was never proven) to have had a romantic relationship.

Evermore's lead single was "Willow," released the same day as the album, December 11. Both album and song debuted at No. 1 in the *Billboard* charts in the same week, and, commercially speaking, "Willow" outshone the album's other two singles by a long way. "No Body, No Crime" reached

No. 34, and the No. 63 placing of "Coney Island" gave it the distinction of being Swift's lowest-charting American single—a record it still holds. Swift said "Willow" was about "casting a spell to make someone fall in love with you," and its finger-picked indie-folk melody was bewitching indeed.

Caught off guard, critics barely had time to listen to the album before assembling their reviews. Especially difficult in that timeframe was picking out salient differences between *Folklore* and *Evermore*: was the latter a continuation of the former, or were they distinct albums with distinct themes? It took a good few listens to establish that *Folklore* felt more sonically cohesive, while *Evermore* is more musically varied. *Evermore*'s songs are also more haunting, with emotions explored in greater depth. See, for example, the hopeless bleakness of "Coney Island": the lights are extinguished, the amusement park is shuttered and Swift is full of heartache about the relationship that has just ended. *Folklore*, by contrast, was less about her own life than about other people's, such as the love-triangle characters invented for "Betty," "Cardigan," and "August."

There would be no new music until *Midnights* came along nearly two years later. In the meantime, Swift had her *Taylor's Versions* to be getting on with (*Fearless*, out in April 2021, was followed that November by *Red*). While fans waited, her pair of sister albums—the definitive pandemic albums—continued to provide comfort.

CHAPTER 14

Midnights

I f *Midnights* offered any headline news, it was this: Pop Taylor was back. Having reinvented herself on *Folklore* and *Evermore* as an auteur—and picked up a substantial new listenership composed of people who hadn't thought she was "worth" hearing before—she had emerged from the folklorian woods. (One has to wonder how this affected new fans who were hoping she would stay in those woods for another few albums.) The electropop that had crackled through the *1989*, *Lover*, and *Reputation* eras was once again her touchstone: the synths and the house beats were back, albeit in an understated way. Written mainly with Jack Antonoff in the twelve-month period starting in autumn 2021, it was a recalibration.

All of this became known only after *Midnights*' release on October 21, 2022. Before it appeared—at midnight, obviously— she'd done no interviews, nor made a single song available in advance. The album simply came out, in its entirety, that night. Saying that, there was what could be called a run-up to release.

Where the folklorian records had arrived with almost no advance notice save a message the day before, this time Swift restored a feeling of anticipation. On August 28, she made an announcement at the MTV Video Music Awards. Accepting the statuette for Best Long Form Video for *All Too Well: The Short Film* (which she wrote and directed), she said: "I thought it might be a fun moment to tell you that my brand-new album comes out October 21."

Note: The impending release of her eleventh album, *The Tortured Poets Department*, was also announced at an awards show. On February 4, 2024, collecting the Grammy for Best Pop Vocal Album for *Midnights*, she said: "I want to say thank you to the fans by telling you a secret that I've been keeping from you for the last two years, which is that my brand-new album comes out on April 19. It's called *The Tortured Poets Department*." In some quarters, the announcement was "controversial" because it was deemed to have "hijacked" the Grammys, and with hindsight, she might have been better off not mentioning *TTPD*.

The reason for that relates to a misjudgment later that evening, when she won—for the fourth time, a record for any artist—Album of the Year. It was presented by Celine Dion, making a rare public appearance since being diagnosed with a neurological disorder, stiff-person syndrome, in 2022. The iconic Dion received a standing ovation when she was escorted on stage by her oldest son, René-Charles—Swift was on her feet, applauding with everyone else—and her stoicism was much in evidence when she stood at the microphone unaided and read out Swift's name as the winner. Swift appeared to be genuinely shocked by her win, which might explain her seemingly "snubbing"—as the media termed it—Dion. Making her way to the stage hand-in-hand with Lana Del Rey, with whom she had duetted on the album track "Snow on the Beach," she exuberantly thanked Jack Antonoff and other *Midnights* collaborators who had joined her onstage; meanwhile, Dion waited several yards away, holding the gramophone trophy. Finally stepping toward her, Swift nodded and smiled her thanks, took the Grammy, and turned back to her friends.

Swift later met Dion backstage, where the two were photographed embracing. All appeared to be well, but seemingly forgetting Dion onstage gave some critics an excuse to also feel offended by the *Tortured Poets Department* announcement. She had "made it all about her"—an affront.

And yet . . . her decision to mention the album can probably be excused as a case of justifiable excitement. There was even a link between *TTPD* and *Midnights*—she started work on the former as soon as she submitted *Midnights* to Republic Records. By the time of the Grammys, she had worked on *TTPD* for nearly two years.

Returning to August 28, 2022, the world was aware that *Midnights* was en route. Between September 21 and October 7, she drip-fed song titles—but no music—via TikTok. On October 17, she ramped up the anticipation by posting a *Midnights* Manifest on Instagram. It took the form of a desk calendar, showing nine days, beginning on October 20 and ending on the 28th. Day 1 offered a handwritten notification that a "Teaser Trailer" would be shown during the "3rd quarter of Thursday Night Football"—and that *Midnights* was due "@ midnight."

The next day, October 21, was filled with album-related activity: "(3 am EST [Eastern Standard Time]) Special very chaotic surprise."

That same day, the video for the lead single, "Anti-Hero," would premiere at 8 a.m. EST, accompanied by a #TSAntiHeroChallenge on YouTube Shorts, and 8 p.m. would bring lyric videos. The box for Saturday, October 22 offered a rather businesslike (or plaintive) request: "stream midnights pls." October 23: "Visit your local record store? stream midnights pls." There were also notations about appearances on Jimmy Fallon's and Graham Norton's chat shows. The 26th and 27th contained more reminders to stream the album and watch the videos.

Swift knew what she was doing: when the chart week ended on October 27, she had sold 1.5 million equivalent chart units, debuting at No. 1, and "Anti-Hero" entered the Hot 100 at No. 1. ("Anti-Hero" also chalked up 17 million first-day streams on Spotify—the highest opening number in the platform's history.) And occupying the No. 2 to No. 10 slots on the Hot 100 were other *Midnights* tracks. She tweeted pithily: "10 out of 10 of the Hot 100??? On my 10th album??? I AM IN SHAMBLES."

Spending eight nonconsecutive weeks at No. 1 in the US—only "Blank Space" came close to its chart-topping success, at seven weeks in 2014–15—"Anti-Hero" remains the biggest single of her career in terms of time spent at No. 1. But in terms of chart-equivalent units—the aggregated figure used by the industry to represent the number of downloads and streams—her undisputed heavyweight champion is "Shake

It Off," which has shifted 10 million units. "Anti-Hero" may or may not eventually exceed that, and there's every chance it will, because it's one of her most-loved songs—a track that manages to be unsparingly self-critical, even self-loathing, yet incredibly catchy. She's, a "narcissist," a "monster"—the lilting, electropop chorus sums it up: it's all her fault. And her honesty ratcheted up her popularity. Swift talked about the song on Instagram a few weeks before it was released. It was one of her favorite songs—not just her favorite track on *Midnights* but one of her favorites of all time. She felt proud of her honesty: "I don't think I've delved this far into my insecurities in this detail this song is a real guided tour throughout all the things I tend to hate about myself."

The "very chaotic surprise" she promised in the manifest turned out to be seven bonus tracks, available on an extended version of the album called *Midnights (3am Edition)*. Meanwhile, the TS Anti-Hero Challenge invited fans to share their "anti-heroic traits." Taylor revealed that her own included thinking that her cat, Benjamin Button, is her son—well, why not?—and being obsessed with the number thirteen.

Midnights was a concept album, inspired by "thirteen sleepless nights scattered throughout my life," she said on social media. Each of its five themes was pretty meaty in its own right: "self-loathing," "fantasizing about revenge," "wondering what might have been," "falling in love," and "falling apart." Taken as a whole, they marked the return of Autobiographical Taylor—her reservations about habitually using a "diaristic" writing style had been put to bed by *Folklore* and *Evermore* and she could now write about her own life again.

Starting with the opening track, in fact. Its title, "Lavender Haze," denoting the state of being in love, was a 1950s term she heard on *Mad Men*. She felt it would serve well as the name of a song about her relationship with Joe Alwyn. But she approached the lyric from the viewpoint of a couple who've spent much of their romance having to ignore social media comments about it. In an Instagram video posted before *Midnights'* release, Swift explained that her own experience of relationships, or at least her then-current one, had been undermined by "weird rumors [and] tabloid stuff" that she and Alwyn dealt with by ignoring them. (The video was removed from Instagram about six months later, after she and Alwyn split.) Like many *Midnights* tracks, it's characterized by a sensual R&B feel and a synthy undertow.

The dreamy "Snow on the Beach" is another relationship track, or rather a track that focuses on the rare phenomenon (so rare that it's akin to snow on the beach) of two people falling in love at the same time. The song was much discussed, because it was her first collaboration with Lana Del Rey, whose cinematic dark-pop is much-loved by Swift. "I think so many female artists would not be where they are and would not have the inspiration they have if it weren't for the work that she's done," she said at the Grammys, as Del Rey watched from several feet away, smiling enigmatically next to Sam Dew, one of the co-writers of "Lavender Haze." "I think she's a legacy artist, a legend in her prime right now. I'm so lucky to know you and be your friend."

Del Rey's contribution to "Snow on the Beach" was considered by some listeners to be so minimal that she was more a backing singer than a 50/50 duet collaborator—enough of them made their feelings known that Swift tweeted on May 24, 2023: "You asked for it, we listened: Lana and I went back into the studio specifically to record more Lana on 'Snow on the Beach.'" She was as good as her word: the new version, with the credit "Feat. More Lana Del Rey," was an equal, glimmering partnership.

The "revenge fantasy" she promised when discussing the album before release was "Vigilante Shit"—the first time she'd used a four-letter word in a title, which provoked a number of articles along the lines of "Taylor Swift Is Cursing More in Her Lyrics Now" (as published on the CinemaBlend site). If the subject of the track was Scooter Braun—as speculated by some fans—the "cursing" showed that she was not ready to call a truce. For what it was worth, in an interview shortly before *Midnights* was released, Braun told podcast host Jay Williams that he regretted the enmity caused by his acquisition of Big Machine. "I made the assumption that everyone, once the deal was done, was going to have a conversation with me, see my intent, see my character and say: 'Great, let's be in business together.'" It was, he added, "a learning lesson."

Three singles were released during the *Midnights* era: "Anti-Hero," of course, but also "Lavender Haze" and "Karma," and the latter could be read as another vengeful moment. On it, she reflects that she has attracted good karma—as reflected by the many blessings in her life—while those who have "betrayed" her have accrued the opposite. A remix of the track features rapper Ice Spice, and that version was nominated for the Best Pop Duo/Group Performance at the 2024 Grammys.

All that remained was for her to bring the album to the public, in person. Having not toured since Reputation wrapped in 2018, Swift had spent the past four years coping with a void where a stadium tour should have been. For months before *Midnights*' release, she'd been working behind the scenes to change that. On November 1, 2022, the *Los Angeles Times* broadcast glad tidings: "Swifties, rise! Taylor Swift is taking *Midnights* on the road with US stadium tour." The tour, Swift announced on *Good Morning America* the same day, was to be known as the Eras Tour. "I'm so excited that I get to look you guys in the eye and say thank you for everything," she said. It had been an "incredible" week, with *Midnights* hitting No. 1 (it would be 2022's top-selling album, despite being released only two months before the end of the year) and her album tracks colonizing the entire Top 10. The Eras Tour would transform her from an everyday superstar-next-door to, as *Elle* put it, "a pop megastar at celestial echelons."

CHAPTER 15

Eras

Dubbed "the greatest show on earth" by the concert-industry magazine *Pollstar*, the Eras Tour began life as a modest run of twenty-seven stadiums over five months. That was what was advertised on the original tour poster, along with a list of opening acts that included Haim, Paramore, and Phoebe Bridgers. It was scheduled to start in Glendale, Arizona, on March 18, 2023, and conclude in Los Angeles on August 5, and would see Swift take "a journey through all of my musical eras of my career," as she said on *Good Morning America*. European dates would soon be announced, she added.

Eras, of course, grew into a 152-show, twenty-one-month globe-spanning phenomenon. Among the many records it has so far broken is that of the highest grossing tour of all time, at $1.039 billion, and along with that came another, unintended, achievement: demand for tickets, described as "unprecedented" by Ticketmaster, crashed its website when it began its presale phase on November 15 (it was scheduled to open to the general public three days later). Fans were eligible for the presale if they'd signed up to Ticketmaster's Verified Fan program between November 1 and 9. Of the 3.5 million hopefuls who did, 1.5 million were sent a code that should have guaranteed them tickets; the other 2 million were put on a waiting list.

Code-holders logged in at 10 a.m. on November 15, expecting to purchase their tickets. Not so fast, Swifties. They were confronted with long waits, glitches that canceled some sales just as the buyer reached the check-out stage and outright crashes of the site. Nevertheless, 2 million tickets were sold— so many that Ticketmaster was left with "insufficient remaining ticket inventory" and canceled the November 18 public sale.

Politicians weighed in: House of Representatives member Alexandria Ocasio-Cortez tweeted on November 15 that Ticketmaster was a "monopoly" that needed to be "reigned [*sic*] in," while Tennessee's attorney general Jonathan Skrmetti vowed to ensure that no consumer protection laws had been broken by the presale trouble.

After canceling the public sale, Ticketmaster explained that although only 1.5 million codes had been issued, 14 million people, which included bots, had tried to access the presale on November 15. However, on November 17, Senator Amy Klobuchar, chair of the Senate Antitrust Committee, wrote to Live Nation, Ticketmaster's parent company since 2010, to express "serious concern about the state of competition in the ticketing industry." And a highly annoyed Swift spoke her mind about the fiasco. Tweeting on November 18, she said her team had asked Ticketmaster "multiple times" whether it could cope with the demand, and were assured it could. It had been "excruciating for me to just watch mistakes happen with no recourse" and she was looking into how to improve the process in the future.

Fans had other things on their minds apart from ticketing chaos. There was frenzied speculation about what the concert setlist would contain, and fans swapped dream lists. Many assumed that because she played nineteen songs on the Reputation Tour, she would do the same on Eras. Never try to second-guess The Swift: she packed in forty-four.

Forty-four songs, ten "acts," sixteen costume changes (accomplished at high velocity—it took just one minute and twenty seconds to shrug off the lilac ballgown worn for the *Speak Now* section and whip on the T-shirt and fedora—as originally seen in the "22" video—that represented the next section, *Red*), three hours, and 70,000 overjoyed fans every night. Nine of the acts were album eras, taking in every album except the debut—no explanation has been proffered, but it could be linked to *Taylor Swift*'s low streaming numbers, as mentioned in Chapter 13; perhaps Swift was just minded to concentrate on more popular eras. On the very first night, in Glendale, however, she did play "Tim McGraw" during the "surprise" slot.

The tenth act was a two-song acoustic section that was intended to change every night, with no duplication. After nearly a year, she ran out of unplayed songs in Australia and began to substitute mash-ups of already visited tunes. Naturally, nobody minded, but Swift, who considers the effect of every tiny alteration, wanted to explain the change. She told the

Melbourne audience on February 18: "I want to be as creative as possible with the acoustic set moving forward. I don't want to limit anything and say, 'Oh, if I've played a song before I can't play it again.'"

Reviews of the tour were near-unanimous raves. It's hard to think of another concert tour that has received this many five-star ovations, this many genuinely awed plaudits. "A completely engrossing three-and-a-half hours of pure joy," said the *Guardian*; "a showcase of the range and versatility that have made Swift the most successful singer-songwriter in an age defined by hip-hop," offered the *Los Angeles Times*; Slant perceptively commented: "People weren't here for something as pedestrian as a concert. They came for a world-shifting event."

When the film *Taylor Swift: The Eras Tour* came out on October 13, write-ups were virtually the same: acknowledgment of her talent and open-mouthed awe at the scale of the event found their way into nearly every review. In the film's first weekend in North America, it took $92.8 million, and another $30.7 million internationally, making it the highest grossing concert film in history. Some industry watchers think it will become one of the most successful films of any genre. Swift and her team's share of the profits said to be around 57 percent, minus a distribution fee for the cinema chain that released it.

Originally scheduled to open on October 13—chosen because of the "13," naturally—Swift unexpectedly moved the date to the 12th in North America. "Look what you genuinely made me do," she wrote on Instagram. "Due to unprecedented demand we're opening up early access showings of *The Eras Tour Concert Film* on THURSDAY in America and in Canada!! As in . . . TOMORROW." The date remained the 13th in the rest of the world.

Moreover, *Eras*' release occasioned a flurry of changes to other films' opening dates. Meg Ryan's much-anticipated rom-com return, *What Happens Later*, and Pete Davidson's *Dumb Money* were among the October 13 releases that were moved to new dates rather than be sent into battle with *Eras*. The most prominent mover was *The Exorcist: Believer*, the internet had dreamed up the tag "ExorSwift" for the double-bill duel, and the industry foresaw an outcome similar to the July 2023 "Barbenheimer" phenomenon (when *Barbie* and *Oppenheimer* played at the same cinemas to the enormous benefit of both). Unfortunately for those who were looking forward to it, *Exorcist* producer Jason Blum rescheduled his opening to October 6. He tweeted waggishly: "Look what you made me do. *The Exorcist: Believer* moves to 10/6/23. #TaylorWins." Blum was good-natured about it, but it must have been galling to lose that Friday the 13th release date—"Friday the 6th" just didn't have the same spookiness.

Eras—tour and film—pushed Swift's net financial worth over the billion-dollar mark. It had been hovering just below that, but Eras took it to $1.1 billion in Bloomberg's "conservative" estimate. That doesn't include the value of her songwriting catalog if she ever sells it, which would add around another $1 billion. To put that in perspective, the most valuable catalog to date has been Bruce Springsteen's, which he sold in 2021 for a reported $550 million.

The handful of other billionaire musicians includes Paul McCartney, Jay-Z, and, rather surprisingly, the late country star

Jimmy "Margaritaville" Buffett, who amassed most of his wealth from non-music ventures like restaurants and his own beer brand. Similarly, Jay-Z, hip-hop's first billionaire and currently the world's wealthiest musician, made a good deal of his $2.5 billion from business interests, including champagne and cognac brands and real estate. Swift, on the other hand, is one of the few ultra-rich to have earned her fortune almost entirely through music. Almost—she's also accumulated a property portfolio said to be worth $150 million.

Because she's never happier than when working unfathomably hard, she found time during Eras to release the next two *Taylor's Version* albums. *Speak Now* came out on July 7, the day Eras reached Kansas City. Her re-recordings of its fourteen original tracks and two of the *Deluxe Edition* tunes were accompanied by six previously unreleased From the Vault tracks. It reached No. 1 in the US and the UK, as did the next re-recording, *1989*, when it made its appearance on October 27. (The original *1989* came out on October 27, 2014—exactly nine years before *Taylor's Version*.)

In the UK, *1989 (TV)* outsold the rest of the Top 10 combined in its first week, at 184,000 "chart units." Of those, nearly 62,000 were on vinyl—a jaw-dropping figure in 2023. For good measure, a previously unreleased *1989* track, "Is It Over Now?," topped the UK singles chart the same week.

During its opening week in America, meanwhile, the album did a good deal more than merely outsell the other Top 10 LPs. *Forbes* said its 1.653 million equivalent units were more than the combined total sold by numbers 2 through 50. Vinyl sales alone totaled 580,000—the highest one-week vinyl figure in the US since the analytics platform Luminate began following sales in 1991. By way of comparison, the album in the No. 2 slot, *Seventeenth Heaven* by South Korean boy band Seventeen, managed 100,000 equivalent units—one-sixteenth of *1989 (TV)*'s sales. In any other week, 100,000 would be more than respectable, but Seventeen were up against not only the biggest artist in the world but one savvy enough to add five unreleased "From the Vault" songs to the tracklisting—making it an absolute must-buy. Swift stoked interest even further by commenting on Instagram: "[T]he 5 From the Vault tracks are so insane. I can't believe they were ever left behind."

Note also that No. 3 that week was Drake's *For All the Dogs*, which came out on October 6, two weeks before *1989 (TV)*. Also one of the world's biggest music names, he undoubtedly expected his album to debut at No. 1, which it obligingly did. But it sold only 402,000 equivalent units in its first week—a quarter of Swift's first-week total. Remarkably, six weeks later, Drake put out a brand-new song that referred directly to Swift's dominance of the chart. Titled "Red Button," it was the first track of *For All the Dogs Scary Hours Edition*, a six-song add-on to his current album. He said she was the only artist he saw as a sales rival, adding that he had delayed his previous album—a joint release with 21 Savage, *Her Loss*—to put distance between it and her 2022 LP, *Midnights*. *Her Loss* had been scheduled for October 28, but when Swift surprise-dropped *Midnights* on October 21, Drake decided to hold his record over until November 4, when Swift's momentum would have slowed. It paid off: *Her Loss* debuted at No. 1 on the US album chart.

The five *TV* Vault tracks were recorded when she made the original *1989* but hadn't made it onto the final tracklist. They languished on the cutting-room floor as *1989* went out into the world and definitively started Swift's ascent to iconhood. The Vault songs finally got their chance to shine when *Taylor's Version* was being put together. Each of her re-recorded albums has featured up to six previously unreleased songs; *1989*'s were "Is It Over Now?"—which, as mentioned, was a No. 1 British single—"Now That We Don't Talk," "Say Don't Go," "Suburban Legends," and "Slut!"

Each had its merits: "Say Don't Go" brims with breathy drama as she mulls over a situationship she's fallen into; the synthy soundbed of "Suburban Legends" is pure, pleasurable 1980s, though the doomed-high school-romance storyline is Taylor by rote—she's frequently written about male infidelity and doesn't have much to add here, apart from a marvelous line about a boyfriend's kiss being so profound that she'll never get over it.

The sparkling "Now That . . ." is considered by many to be about Harry Styles. Clues include a disparaging line about the song's subject letting his hair get long—which Styles did—and another about him testing out new identities. You can almost see her rolling her eyes at that: the One Directioner was just eighteen when they dated, while Swift was twenty-three and a ten-year music industry veteran. The song mourns the end of the affair but also sees the silver lining: they may not be together any more, but at least Taylor no longer has to fake enthusiasm for the music he likes. Swift has no rival when it comes to tiny, universally relatable observations.

The tense, thrumming "Is It Over Now?" is also said to be about Styles—their two-month liaison ran out of steam in January 2013, during a New Year's holiday in the British Virgin Islands which saw Swift going home early. For his part, Styles later attributed their split to the incessant attention they had attracted, and simply to being eighteen and inexperienced at being in a high-profile relationship.

But there was only one Vault pick that inspired articles and analysis everywhere from *The New York Times* to Just Jared: "Slut!" Deceptively dreamy-sounding—if you didn't listen to the lyric, you would assume it was a love song—it reveals what it was like to be on the receiving end of the media's unflagging attempts to slut-shame her. It's not hard to find bemusing examples of that: for instance, the site The Talko ran a listicle story in February 2017 titled "15 Reasons Why It's Dangerous to Date Taylor Swift"; reasons ranged from "She will get too serious too quickly" to "She will probably stray." A later story characterized her as "a female serial dater" and printed pictures of "the sixteen dudes [she] has dated."

"Slut!" addressed the tenor of those articles, but it *was* a love song—when she wrote it, she was happily involved with someone, and the track is a defiant middle finger to anyone who felt inclined to criticize her. It's a strong song and was a serious contender for a place on the original *1989* tracklist. What edged it out? She'd written another song about the media's coverage of her dating life, "Blank Space," and felt the latter was more in keeping with the general feel of the album. Good call.

In a typically Swiftian visual joke, she picked August 9, 2023, to announce that *1989 (Taylor's Version)* was coming in the autumn. Written in the American style—month followed by day—August 9 is 8/9. (The trick loses its impact slightly using the UK system, which makes the date 9/8, but either way the method of the announcement underscored her bond with the Swifties.) Their devotion is repaid by Swift's own loyalty to them; there's endless badinage between Swift and the Swifties. Not for nothing were tickets for *The Eras Tour* film $19.89 for adults and $13.13 for children.

It hardly needs saying that virtually all purchasers of *Taylor's Version* owned the original *1989*, but the re-recording was, for any fan, a compulsory addition to their collection. Buying it was, first of all, a direct way of supporting the re-record project. But buyers didn't have to be motivated by loyalty alone— Swift made it worth their while to part with cash. When fans went to her web store or a real-life record shop, they found eleven physical editions of the album, which came with posters or Polaroids. There were CDs and vinyl LPs in four different colors, and even a cassette version reflecting the retro format's increasing popularity with Gen Z.

Many Swifties are completists, buying every format of a release, and in this instance they were catered to. "There's a reason Taylor Swift is a billionaire," *Variety* wryly wrote. And yet, who could resist the lure of owning the full set of colors, just because their names are so appealing? There's a Sunrise Boulevard Yellow, a Rose Garden Pink, an Aquamarine Green, *and* a Crystal Skies Blue, each of them prettily rendered in the palest pastel. A limited-edition Tangerine version, available only in Target stores in the US, also appeared. (Sunrise yellow, aquamarine, and tangerine are all mentioned in the lyrics to

"Slut!") All sold out and, inevitably, some quickly reappeared on eBay. As of this writing, a bundle of all five vinyl LPs was offered on eBay for $359.70. For comparison, on Swift's own online store, a single vinyl record was $31.89. If all five were available, they would cost $159.45.

Swifties new and old were thrilled when Taylor announced a new album to be released in early 2024. For a record she'd managed to keep secret for two years, *The Tortured Poets Department* made a huge amount of noise once it appeared. There may have been people who had no opinion about it, but they were massively outnumbered by the millions who had something to say. In the weeks following its release, the subject of Swift was almost literally unavoidable, in both mainstream and social media.

Billboard named it the first album to reach 1 billion Spotify streams in a week; equally remarkably, during that first week it sold 1.9 million copies, either physical or downloaded, and of that number 859,000 were vinyl (worth pointing out, because that kind of vinyl sale is reminiscent of the format's 1970s heyday). It hardly needs saying that it debuted at No. 1 in the US, the UK, Australia, New Zealand, Norway, and Sweden, to name just a few. (Its first single, "Fortnight," featuring a toned-down Post Malone, also topped the chart in America, Britain, and elsewhere.) Reviewers scrambled to assemble their thoughts about the music—only allowed to hear it the night before release, they had to make up their minds on the spot and come up with lengthy meditations about it.

Luckily, Swift gave them a lot to work with. In spring 2023, soon after splitting with Joe Alwyn, she'd had a brief but apparently profound (at least from her perspective) relationship with Matty Healy of The 1975. Known for occasionally off-color behavior, he was an unpopular choice with her family and Swifties alike, and the track "But Daddy I Love Him" defiantly tells them to mind their own business. "I Can Fix Him (No Really I Can)" and the out-and-out diss track "The Smallest Man Who Ever Lived" address the evident hopelessness of their fling. Alwyn, meanwhile, is a more low-key figure on the album. The string-accented "So Long, London," which alludes to the desolation of a relationship on its last legs, is the track seemingly most inspired by him, but the deceptively bubbly "I Can Do It With a Broken Heart" and a pounding duet with Florence + The Machine, "Florida!!!," also appear to reference the person she once considered the love of her life (the first initial of "loml," an elegiac ballad, stands for both "love" and "loss").

Reviews were broadly positive, praising Swift's unfailing poeticism and her talent for capturing the "chaos" and "revelry"—as she put it in "But Daddy I Love Him"—of a love affair, especially an affair that's hit the rocks. (Note: unofficial sweatshirts with the slogan "Chaos + Revelry" were available online within days of *TTPD*'s release.) If *TTPD* had weaknesses, they were generally agreed to be its length—thirty-one tracks, counting its surprise-released second half, *The Anthology*—and a sense that her creative partnership with Jack Antonoff, who co-produced most of the first half and part of the second (Aaron Dessner oversaw the rest), had grown tired. *Rolling Stone*'s comment: "At a certain point, it begins to feel as though Swift and Antonoff are simply going through the motions," was echoed by a number of critics. Another *Rolling Stone* reviewer, however, was more beguiled, writing: "Come for the torture, stay for the poetry."

As for *The Eras Tour* film, it's a straightforward capture of her Eras set (the tour is due to wrap up in Vancouver on December 8, five days before her thirty-fifth birthday), albeit shortened from the live set's 195 minutes to 169 and shorn of half a dozen songs. Conceived by Swift herself, it was aimed at two groups of fans: those who couldn't get tickets for a live Eras date, and the luckier ones who did see the show but wanted to watch it again, this time catching details they'd missed in the frenzy of the live gig.

For both, *The Eras Tour* is almost as good as the real thing. In some ways it's even better. *People* called it a "Tay-quake," and that seems about right. While the drawback of *Eras* is that it doesn't replicate the headiness of being in the same room as 70,000 other crying, singing Swifties—joining in with the communal spirit is a non-negotiable part of attending a Swift show—it takes watchers right onto the stage, inches from Swift. We see the tiniest things: her hair dampening with sweat, the individual sequins on her gowns, the intricacies of her choreography.

And we look at the audience from her perspective. For the past fifteen years, what Taylor has seen when she looks out from the stage is pinpricks of light—tens of thousands of people holding up phones. As soon as she became a headline act, she was booked into large venues, which almost uniformly sold out. So, from 2009's Fearless Tour onward, her onstage experience has been a detached one, defined by the lights of smartphones recording the show.

(Note: She had a slower start in the UK, where she played her first gigs at London's 2,000-capacity Shepherd's Bush Empire on May 6 and 7, 2009. Though both shows were sold out, they'd been crammed into Fearless's itinerary, between Biloxi, Mississippi, and Spokane, Washington, where she'd performed for 9,436 and 10,798 fans, respectively. By comparison, the London shows were tiny—and it must have been their small scale that caused a *Guardian* critic to comment a year later, in a review of Lady Antebellum, that they were "likely to remain a niche interest [in the UK], like contemporaries Taylor Swift and Rascal Flatts.")

So, Swift's view of her concert crowds has long been one that only the biggest stars have experienced, but now, as shown in *Eras*, it's surreally detached. The fans are out there and, due to LED bracelets given to each as they enter the venue, every one of them sparkles. Yet the woman they've come to see, whose songs are among the most personal and intimate in pop, is physically distanced from them. *Eras* offers a taste of that. The SoFi Stadium in Inglewood, where it was filmed, looks gorgeous and jewellike as the wristbands twinkle, and Swift must appreciate it from an aesthetic viewpoint, but it also highlights the loneliness of her position. "Loneliness" doesn't refer to her offstage life, which is filled with companionship and love, but to the fact that so few people can relate to what she sees from a concert stage.

An unlikely but helpful comparison is Bon Jovi. The New Jersey rockers know exactly what it's like to play the world's biggest stages, and while touring the 1995 album *These Days*, they allowed a handful of competition winners to share the sensation each night. The fans were escorted onstage during the show and seated on the left side in a spot that was set up with chairs and tables to resemble a local dive bar. It was only a few yards from where the band was playing. A few songs later, they returned to their seats in the audience, having had both the thrill of a lifetime and an insight into the onstage experience of a stadium act.

The *Guardian* covered their show at Munich's Olympia-stadion in June that year. Their writer was allowed to watch from the onstage bar—and found it daunting to be seen by 75,000 people, even though every one of them was looking only at Jon Bon Jovi. "The crowd out there is horrifyingly vast. Mercifully, everyone beyond the first few rows blurs into a blancmange of waving arms," the reviewer wrote. "A banner draped over a crash barrier announces, 'Jon, we will wait for you,' or something similar; the view is partly obscured by spotlights trained on the stage from about half a mile away."

This is essentially what Swift sees every time she sets foot on a concert stage. Some megastars might use similar moments to reflect on what a lonely game fame can be. Swift, though, has reached the summit of twenty-first-century culture, secure in the knowledge that she's surrounded by love. If she ever worries that she's not "enough" as she is—it happens to all of us—she can look out at the crowd every night and know that her work as a musician matters deeply to them. Her music has changed their lives. So, when she sends out love each night, singing to every fan, from those in the front row to those in the furthest corner, she feels the love returned a millionfold.

Acknowledgments

Many thanks to Lucy Stewardson, my fantastic editor at Michael O'Mara Books, and to Annie Zaleski and super-Swiftie Gian Gnaegi, both of whom were generous with their expert knowledge.

Thank you to *Billboard*, Bloomberg, CMT, *Elle*, *Entertainment Weekly*, *Esquire*, *Forbes*, Great American Family, the *Guardian*, *The New York Times*, the *New York Daily News*, *Pollstar*, *Rolling Stone*, Salon.com, and *Variety*.

And much appreciation to *Journey to Fearless*, *A Place in This World*, *Miss Americana*, *Bobbycast* podcast, @taylorswift13 on X/Twitter, @taylorswift on Instagram, Taylor Swift on MySpace, @robertellisorrall on Instagram, @CalvinHarris on X/Twitter, and @kellyclarkson on X/Twitter.

Picture Credits

The publishers would like to thank the following sources for their kind permission to reproduce the pictures in this book.

Plate photographs in order of appearance:

Every effort has been made to acknowledge correctly and contact the source and/or copyright holder of each picture, and the publisher apologizes for any unintentional errors or omissions, which will be corrected in future editions of this book.

Index